PIANO TECHNIQUE DEMYSTIFIED

Insights into Problem Solving

**A Practical Syllabus for Student, Teacher and Performer
with Photos, Examples from the Repertoire and
Fifty Teaching Moments**

NEIL STANNARD

NoSuchThing Press 2013
First Edition
All Rights Reserved
ISBN: 9781482799705

My students made me do this.
I thought it was impossible, yet here it is.
So, this book is for them.

And for Karen,
who knew first-hand that life wasn't fair.
1955-2013

CONTENTS

MUSICAL EXAMPLES

Unlike life, playing the piano is easy and doesn't hurt.

INTRODUCTION

READ THIS FIRST

When I was a young piano student the best advice offered me was to practice slowly, practice in rhythms and do this repeatedly. Never was it explained to me how slowly to practice or why. Nor was I told the point of practicing in rhythms. In fact, never was the concept of practicing explained to me at all. I learned a four-octave routine in which I could rattle off major and minor scales in octaves, sixths and tenths. But once I had it down, something in me rejected that route as a way of life. I realize now that my instinct saved me a great deal of time. Of course, like most anxious children who tend to be intimidated by authority, I was at a loss for words, particularly in the form of a question. I don't recall ever asking a question, except once when I came across a mordent symbol for the first time.

A certain facility came quickly and easily to me, which may explain why I escaped more rigorous incursions by teachers into my private musical world. Czerny studies were offered, though as I recall, not stressed with particular enthusiasm. From rather early on, ever more advanced repertoire passed through my hands and, exciting as that was for an eager musical mind, problems would abound and my instinct was to pass over, play through or otherwise ignore them. Somehow I made the music convincing enough to pass inspection, at least for a time, but I always felt at the mercy of the piano and its mysteries. There appeared more and more brick walls and by the time I reached collage, my forehead was quite sore.

I was definitely not a prodigy. Facile sight-reading, physical dexterity and the emotional outpourings of the neurotic loner made up my skill set. When I practiced, and I use the term here loosely, technical passages sounded best on the first few readings. The more I repeated them the worse they got. Strange, no? You may be wondering how I handled this phenomenon. Simple, I practiced less and played more.

Did you spot the clue I planted in the previous paragraph? If so, you may have a head start on the material in this book. If passages get worse on repetition, that is, if the mechanism tires and accuracy or speed become forfeit, then muscles are not working in an efficient, well-synchronized manner. Back up now to the first paragraph. When I got serious about perfecting a movement, and I was a very serious student, all I knew to do was repeat slowly and in various rhythms. All that this produced, sadly, was a working-in of technical vagaries, perhaps correct and useful or wrong and destructive. Fortunately, since my practicing consisted primarily of playing, I escaped injury.

The advice given to me about practicing is akin to a doctor treating a patient without an examination. No doctor would prescribe all of his remedies to every patient for every ailment, regardless of the complaint. The advice is too general and vague. It comes from an approach that assumes muscles are muscles and if you build them technique will come. This is not true.

A pharmacist friend of mine spent most of his career observing the inner workings of the pharmaceutical industry. He has developed a somewhat cynical attitude, justifiable I think, regarding the development of remedies. Many pills go through many trials and are often rejected for their intended purposes. What then to do with these pills? Obviously, invent a disease. I offer here some remedies, but if you don't have the ailment, don't invent one. Every pianist comes from a different technical background in which some, perhaps most, of the technique works just fine. My purpose here is to describe as well as words will allow what the body can do, what it wants to do and how to put it to use in the service of making music at the piano.

You can't learn to play the piano just from a book and you can't teach someone to play the piano without one. (I'm tempted to add that you can't teach the piano without *this* book, but that would be immodest.) For the student, this book can be the key to unlocking mysteries of technique; it can show the way to making a seemingly difficult passage ridiculously easy to play. For the teacher, this book can be a reference point, a place to find answers and discover ways to present solutions to both technical and musical problems. For students and teachers together, the information in these pages will help to demystify the process of learning *how to practice* (see Chapter Five) so that the act of making music is a joyous one, devoid of physical struggle and discomfort. How can anyone make music while enduring torture? And in the process you will learn how to learn anything.

Organized around specific questions brought to me from my applied students at the University of Texas at El Paso and at my private studios in New York City and Los Angeles, you will find here a distillation of what I have learned during a lifetime of teaching and playing the piano and performing in public. Notice the distinction between *playing the piano* and *performing in public* (see Chapter Fifteen).

This is not, of course, a comprehensive plan for building a technique with every possible refinement described in detail. It is, rather, a source of information on a wide variety of topics pertinent to pianists. You may find that some topics require more study than others in order to grasp their concepts, but I promise the effort is worthwhile. It is not necessary to read the chapters in any particular order. You can, if you like, dip in at whatever topic seems relevant to your particular needs at the moment. Working with a teacher who can demonstrate the movements I'll be describing is very helpful. If such a person is not available, the topics on technique you read about here will serve as an introduction to the world of efficient playing and you will take with you, at the very least, the notion that if a passage doesn't feel easy or if it causes you worry, it hasn't been completely solved. You will learn not to accept a so-so execution. You will learn that knowledge is available and there is no mystery.

All of my teachers have contributed in varying degrees to my collection of methods and remedies and it is impossible sometimes to make attributions. I do remember Muriel Kerr, though, saying that "sound is our business" and from this I felt a vague nudge in the direction of voicing for color. But only a nudge. Nothing was said about *how* to voice. If I remember correctly, her comment was in response to my complaint about a beast of an instrument I had just played, expecting sympathy and getting only a shrug and something like "we're pianists and sound is our business." Later, when I suggested to a conductor that he engage Kerr for a concerto, he told me he'd invited her many times but she only played Steinway and they didn't have one. I loved and admired her, but Kerr's point of view comes under the category "do as I say, not as I do." In these pages you won't find any recommendation that isn't a part of my own regimen.

Jacob Gimpel, another superior performer, once said my Liszt E-flat concerto was ready for performance in an upcoming European tour with a youth orchestra, but that my playing wasn't completely honest. He assigned Cramer etudes as a remedy, saying that Cramer was a compliment, from which I gathered that Czerny would have been an insult. Well, my artistic temperament inclines toward accepting a negative as the truth, rather more so than a positive. So, I left his studio that day, head bowed, believing that my playing was dishonest, but without a clue as to what that meant pianistically. And it never occurred to me to ask. So, I'd like to make it clear that questions are a good thing and always appropriate. If a student asks *why* he or she should do something a certain way and the teacher doesn't have an answer, the student should ask for his money back. Later in this book we'll consider whether studies such as those offered by Czerny and Cramer lead to pianistic honesty.

Though my teachers have been many and I am grateful to them all, the one who propelled me with the greatest ease and conviction into a lifetime of joyous music making was Edna Golandsky, who, nearly forty years ago, removed the mystery and provided answers. I had already accumulated advanced degrees in music and embarked on a performing career as a collaborative pianist when quite by chance I discovered her teaching. I don't recommend changing technique with a performance of the Kreutzer Sonata pending at Carnegie Recital Hall, but better that than not finding out important truths about the art that is to dominate one's life. It was during my time with Golandsky that I learned about the business of sound. I learned *what* color at the piano could be. And it was during this time that I began to realize what Gimpel had tried to say. I learned *why* my playing might have been considered dishonest and *how* to fix it.

The principles of how to think about music and physical movement that I have learned from others over the years have become my own, refined and polished from constant use. Physiology, however, has not changed. The muscles, ligaments and tendons of every student's playing apparatus remain unchanged and probably will remain so for at least several more millennia. It is particularly important, therefore, to consider thoughtfully the nature of the playing apparatus and its needs. All questions of movement at the keyboard should be answered in light of what we know about the body's design and its most efficient use. Our goal is to solve technical problems by using the body's design fluidly, that is, by allowing it to function naturally. And this is the central issue of our work here. But how do we know what is a natural movement and what is not without studying medicine, or at least anatomy? Read on.

ONE

ANATOMY FOR PIANISTS

FOREARM ROTATION

No big words. No names of body parts. All you need to know, practically speaking, and I'm going out on a limb here (no pun intended), is that no parts of the playing apparatus should tire or ever experience pain. Leave the tension in the emotional content of the sound you make; don't allow it to take up residence in your body. Making music should feel easy. If it doesn't, then the underlying physical issues have not been solved. Period.

Well, almost. It *is* important to know about the forearm and how it contributes to playing the piano. All pianists use a movement called *forearm rotation* whether they realize it or not. This is a movement that we were designed to make. We know this because it is easy to do, very efficient and not tiring. (I don't want to look at any x-rays, thank you.) And fortunately for us, the body will take a natural movement over an unnatural one, e.g., stretching to an extreme, if we give it a chance. Keep in mind, though, that muscle memory is powerful, and sometimes a period of retraining is required. Try this:

> Drop an arm to your side. Now, raise it from the elbow. No, not like that. Don't turn your arm so that your hand is over the keys. Just raise your arm up from the elbow so that your hand is in the karate-chop position. This would be the position of your hand *without* forearm rotation. *Now* turn (rotate) your hand in the direction of your thumb so that your hand can rest on the keys in a playing position.

The simple movement you just made is a rotation of the forearm, the fastest movement we have, and it is impossible to play the piano without it. In fact, the forearm is constantly rotating toward the thumb just to keep the hands on the keys. This movement gives us power and speed, assists in the achievement of leaps and underlies virtually every move we make at the keyboard. For a somewhat embryonic description, see Tobias Matthay, *On the Visible and Invisible in Pianoforte Playing.* Others have written about this concept as well, namely Georgy Sandor in *On Piano Playing*. But the most useful and comprehensive understanding of the importance of forearm rotation comes from Dorothy Taubman's research, which is, as of this writing, available in DVD form under the title *Virtuosity in a Box*. Notice how many words it took to describe forearm rotation. This is why I say that you can't learn to play just from a book.

The most obvious applied examples of forearm rotation in music occur in so-called *Alberti* figures. These are patterns of pitches that change direction with every note, the ubiquitous accompaniment patterns found in Classical piano pieces and elsewhere. Here it is in the left-hand pattern of Mozart's piano sonata in C Major, K. 545:

Example 1-1 Mozart K. 545.
LH Rotation C to G.

Figure 1-3: Start.

Figure 1-4: From C.

Figure 1-5: To Thumb.

Figure 1-6: From G.

These photos (Figures 1-3 to 1-6) show exaggerated forearm rotation in the Mozart Alberti motive of Example 1-1 above. It can be useful to feel the rotation first as a somewhat exaggerated movement in order teach the sensation to the hand and arm. Notice how many photos that took. An in-person demonstration, though fleeting, can perhaps get the concept across more easily. Yet having the stills available, I find, is substantially more useful. Photos of the identical passage played in tempo, that is, without exaggeration, would resemble Figure 1-3 at each note.

Things to remember about forearm rotation:

- It is an underlying tool and not obvious to the viewer in speed. It is obvious to the pianist if it is missing, as it will be difficult to control sound and create even passagework.
- The hand and arm are unified, straight but not rigid, creating an axle reaching from the tip of the active finger to the elbow.
- It is a tool for training the hand-arm relationship to complete the playing of a note. That is, what it feels like to walk from one note to the next.
- The arm rotates away from one note and back to the next note, but the finger lands straight on the key.
- In speed, the fingers are left with the sensation of walking, transferring weight from the bottom of one key to the bottom of the next, but the mechanisms become more general. That is, one no longer thinks of forearm rotation, but rather more general ways to feel the support of the arm behind the finger that is playing.
- Rotation does not act alone, but rather in combination with a shaping movement and a walking arm.

Practice hint: Think waltz and say "swing, play, *stay,*" where *swing* is an upbeat.

Angle of hand in thumb crossing.

Example 1-2 Rotation in C Scale.

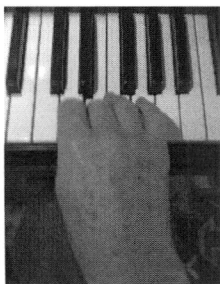

Figure 1-7 Thumb Pulled Under hand. Don't.

Have you heard of the circular piano keys? A company called Neuhaus and Söhne built one in 1882 in order to accommodate the nature of our limbs, presumably to avoid either having to lean to the side or involve upper limbs. It didn't catch on. Well, we've learned to adjust, at least some of us have, to the straight keyboard. As long as we remain in line with ourselves, that is, keeping the forearm straight from the tip of the playing finger to the elbow, we can be at any angle with the piano. That's right, we don't need the circular design. This means that the hand will often be at a slight angle in the direction of the music, particularly in advance of a thumb crossing in a scale, for example. The thumb hangs approximately behind the finger that is playing, and as the arrows in Example 1-2 indicate, it plays rotationally to the F; it is not pulled under the palm.

Figure 1-8 Angle of Hand w. Thumb on C.

Figure 1-9 Angle of Hand w. 2 on D.

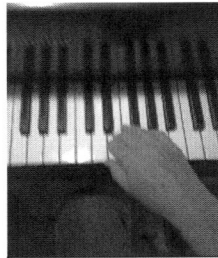

Figure 1-10 Angle of Hand w. 3 on E.

And that's how simple it is. Really. Once the subtleties of its applications are understood and well worked-in, forearm rotation will have you well on your way to virtuosic technique.

Figure 1-11 Angle of Hand as Thumb Prepares to Rotate.

Figure 1-12 Hand after Rotating to F and Clicking into new Position.

Endnotes:
- Forearm rotation underlies all playing.
- It is the way we move from finger to finger, transferring the arm's weight, completing each note as if walking.
- This is how we control the tone.
- This is how we achieve clarity in speed.
- Alignment of finger, hand and arm is essential.
- In a well-coordinated arm, there is no sense of forearm movement.

TWO

IF ROTATION IS ONLY A TOOL, HOW DO WE REALLY MOVE?

SHAPING AND THE WALKING ARM

A student brought Mozart's sonata K. 333 to a lesson, complaining of difficulty playing rhythmically even sixteenth notes in certain passages in the first movement. He proudly announced that he could stretch his hand over the required notes, but no matter how hard he tried, he couldn't control the sound. I cringed at the word *stretched*. Here was a student who didn't yet understand that,

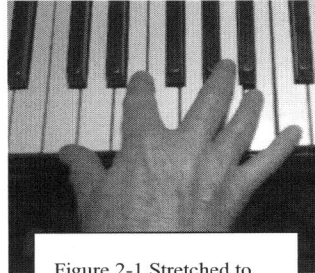

Figure 2-1 Stretched to cover all notes. Don't.

despite what some might see as counter intuitive, it is actually more efficient to move than to stretch to an extreme. The hand can of course be open and flexible, but anytime it is forced to extend to its extreme position, possibilities for efficient activity of the fingers are greatly reduced. This is one of the problems I made for myself years ago, I think, when repetition made passages worse. So, I felt well-qualified to discuss it.

I decided this would be an opportune moment to talk about lateral movements, shaping and its sibling, the walking arm. As we have seen, rotation is our fastest movement and places the arm behind the finger that is playing. But rotation alone won't help us travel up and down the keyboard where intervals exceed the easy range of the hand. This student gleefully showed me that by locking his hand in position he could, in the following example, easily reach the major seventh, C to B, using thumb to fourth finger (Figure 2-1). Since the passage requires repeating the thumb, he instinctively— that is without thinking—kept his thumb extended over the C as he played the upper notes in the figure. This simple, thoughtless act on his part instantly removed any possibility for controlling the action of the fingers into the keys, that is, he no longer was able to support the finger with the weight of the forearm, having cut off his hand from his arm. Yes, almost literally. I fetched a towel to wipe up the blood spatters, calmed the young man and showed him how to reattach his arm.

Example 2-1 Mozart K. 333.

Instead of cutting off his hand from his arm and, indeed, his fingers from his hand, the student should have remembered that the favorite position of the hand is closed. To achieve this feeling, the arm must be behind the finger that is playing. So, gentle reader, you already know the solution to this part of the problem. Yes, he needs first to review the forearm rotation to remind his hand what it feels like to complete each note.

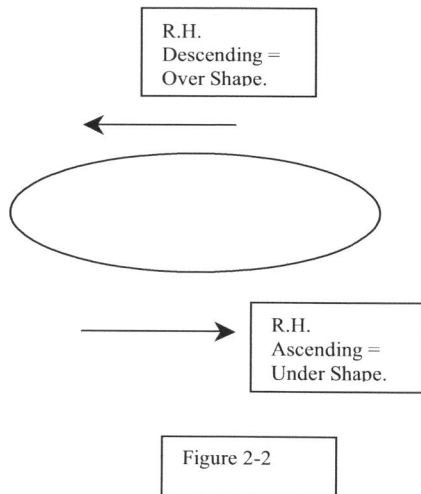

R.H. Descending = Over Shape.

R.H. Ascending = Under Shape.

Figure 2-2

Next, I showed him the essentials of technical shaping, not to be confused with musical shaping, which can be quite different (see Chapter Three, *On Grouping Notes*). For our purposes here, there are two types of shapes, *over* and *under*. This is quite simple: In the right hand, descending passages are shaped *over* and ascending passages are shaped *under*. That is, groups of notes that move together downward in pitch describe a flattened arc *over* to the left and groups of notes that move together upward in pitch describe a flattened arc *under* to the right. (See Figure 2-2.) Since the hands are mirror images of each other, the left hand does the opposite. Notice that the shape described is an ellipse, not a circle, and that there are *no acute angles*. Notice, too, that there are no broken lines, meaning that this movement is *continuous*, no stopping and starting. And as always, how much do you need? Make it as narrow as possible.

Figure 2-3 Start Over Shape From E.

Figure 2-4 Over Shape to Thumb C.

Figure 2-5 On C.

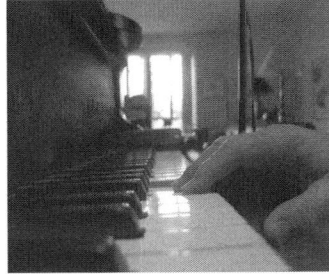

Figure 2-6 Under From Thumb to 4 on B.

Figure 2-7 Starting Over from C (5) to F (2)

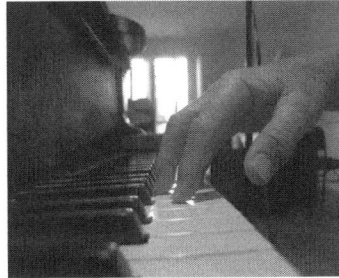

Figure 2-8 On Way Over from C to F.

Figure 2-9 On F.

Figure 2-10 On Way to thumb C. Under Shape Then Starts Over.

The above photos (Figures 2-3 to 2-10) illustrate how the hand looks in motion during over and under shaping. The hand will open during wider intervals, but does not remain so. It is very important to note that the hand is not static, locked in an open position, but rather it is on the way from one note to another in a smooth, flattened ellipse.

And now to debunk an old wives tale, not that I have anything against old wives. It's their constant iteration of myths I don't like. This is not a wrist movement. Repeat: This is not a wrist movement. But—I hear you stammer—my wrist is moving. Yes—I say—I hope it is. But this movement is not *initiated* from the wrist. So, please don't think *wrist* when you shape. The action is initiated from the fingers and hand while we think *over* and *under*, allowing the rest of the apparatus to do what it does, not *making* it do anything. The danger in thinking *wrist* is the disengagement of the fingers.

Here's your assignment: Using a pencil, mark with arcs the *over* and *under* shapes in measure four of Example 2-2, right hand. Look for groups of notes that move in the same direction. Are there any elisions? At what point does the direction change? Will there be an acute angle or is it a continuous motion (see Figure 2-2)? Try it at the piano.

Example 2-2

The walking arm is a little subtler than shaping. Take the above example (2-2) and consider the lateral movement of the hand-arm collaboration when it moves from thumb to the second finger and subsequently from the thumb to the third finger, but within the under shape. The slight opening out of the hand, not stretching to an extreme, is a lateral walking motion. The thumb does not stay on its note, but rather walks on as part of the hand to its new position. We'll have more about this in our discussion of leaps (Chapter Four), but consider now the opening of Chopin's first etude, op. 10, no. 1. Notice how, at first glance, the hand seems to be required to extend over the expanse of a tenth. This is quite a bit of geography to cover for most hands, and without a doubt will create a feeling of being stretched. Do this: 1) Locate the groups (notes that move in the same direction in this case); 2) Shape *under* on the way up with a small *over* on the way down (the

Example 2-3 Chopin Etude Op. 10, 1.

interval of a third); 3) Allow the hand to open, that is, *walk* from thumb to second finger, then close again as it continues toward five by keeping the thumb with your hand. Did you notice how we've combined grouping (Chapter 3), shaping and the walking arm? I know, rather sneaky.

Endnotes:
- Shape *under* or *over*.
- Shape *in* or *out* (Chapter Three).
- Shaping is a more general way to place the arm behind the finger.
- Short finger on short key draws the hand *in*.
- Walk gradually *in* or *out* in order to avoid sudden lurches.

- Move *in* or *out* to facilitate playing of repeated notes.
- Walking arm is a lateral movement.
- Walking arm allows the hand to open in order to give support to the active finger in wider intervals. The thumb and other fingers move with the hand, not extended.

THREE

ON GROUPING NOTES

BIRDS OF A FEATHER

The *technical* grouping of notes can be different from the *musical* or *notational* grouping of notes, although very often there is overlap. An understanding of this idea is crucial to the successful playing of quick passages. You've probably heard the expression, "birds of a feather flock together." Well, consider notes that move in the same direction to be such birds; this is one of the criteria for grouping notes. We often select fingering in order to facilitate such groups of notes, which in turn, can facilitate their execution. In fact, the point at which groups change direction is often one of contention, a place to look when the hand senses something out of order.

In measure two of the following example from Bach's eighth invention, notice how the descending passage in the right hand doubles back on itself by one note. This is an excellent introduction to the concept of grouping. The fourth finger begins each group and the fingers play out until the new group begins. Now, class, how do we get from the thumb back to the fourth finger for the next group? Exactly right. We rotate from the thumb to the fourth finger, and in so doing we avoid the feeling of being crowded, of feeling the thumb and fourth finger pinching together. (There can also be a slight in-out shape, but that's a little later in the chapter.) When practicing, I think of the first note of each group as a mini-starting place, which is felt but not necessarily heard. Can you figure out the groupings for the left hand in measure three of the example?

Example 3-1 Bach Invention No. 8 Grouping Notes in Same Direction.

Chopin creates a more challenging passage in his C-sharp minor etude from opus 10, number 4. Look at the first complete measure in the example below. On each beat there is a changing-note-group, which, beginning on the second beat, would be fingered 3-4-1-2. But since we understand about technical grouping, we know that putting together the notes that move in the same direction might be easier. So, we start our groupings from the thumb and play a series of four-note scales (see arrows in line one of Example 3-2). Try it. It's much easier.

> Group together notes moving in the same direction.

Example 3-2 Chopin Etude, Op. 10 No. 4, Grouping.

Now look at measure three, in which we find groups of notes moving by skips, not by steps. The first three notes move up to E in the same direction and starting again with E, they move down together in the same direction. Again, thinking of these notes as groups, I use them to help give a beginning and ending to shaping, *under* on the way up in pitch and *over* on the way down in pitch (see the arrows on top of line 2 in Example 3-2). Can you see where the arm walks? Look at the intervals in line 2 where the thumb moves to the second finger and where the second finger moves laterally and a little *out* to the fifth finger. The arm is walking as it connects these intervals and keeps the hand feeling closed.

And now, if your brain isn't already full, here's more of that very useful shaping, *in* and *out*, where *in* is in the direction of the fall board and *out* is toward the torso. Notice how in line two of the example the thumb starts on a black key. This automatically puts the hand *in*. The next note, G-sharp with the second finger, is also a black key, but the third note, E with the fifth finger, is on a white key. So, why does this matter? If you allow the hand to move slightly out on the white key, making a very narrow angle from thumb to five, you'll find that the fifth finger has more room to play. Try it. But wait, there's even more. You are now *out* on the fifth finger E, putting the hand in a lovely position to play the next notes, which happen to be white keys, a lateral movement downward in pitch. (What is the shape for moving down?) Are you still with me? This is really neat. The next group, ascending from B-sharp starts on a white key and moves to black keys. Can you visualize the diagram? We've made a diagonal line from *in* (black) to *out* (white), a lateral line down in pitch (white to white) and another diagonal line from *out* (white) to *in* (black). We've made an X with a line through it: X̶.

Notice, if you haven't already, that when we play with short fingers (one and five) on black keys, our hand is drawn *in*. Alternatively, when the long fingers play on black keys the hand can be *out*. Remember, since the keys are actually levers, we have the most control at positions farthest from the fulcrum. So, the loveliest feeling is with the long fingers on short keys and the short fingers on long keys. But of course, unlike the poor string players, we can play virtually anywhere on the key. Try the illustrated passage at the piano: Shaping under and over, shaping in and out, walking arm, visualize the X̶. (I don't mention rotation because, if you recall, it is our underlying tool and, with any luck at all, it has been absorbed so well that it is working in the background, helping to keep the arm behind the finger and keeping us in the key.)

Consider now the example below, Chopin's F-major etude from opus ten. Here all of the notes of the first measure cascade downward in the same direction. Easy, you say, it's one long group. Yes and no, I respond, look closer. Musically, it *is* one long shape. But for technical reasons we group to facilitate a thumb crossing. On the way down, group from the thumb C, using its power to throw the hand across to fourth-finger A. Going up, continue to group from thumb C, taking the thumb with the hand—don't leave it stretched out behind. Keep the hand at an angle in the direction of the music, again using the rotational power of the thumb to click into the new group.

Example 3-3 Chopin Etude Op. 10, No. 8 Grouping

Hand angle

In Chopin's "Winter Wind" etude, the four sextuplets sometimes fall technically into six groups of four (Example 3-4). The thumb's rotation clicks the hand into position for the new

Hand angle

Example 3-4 Chopin Etude Winter Wind. Grouping

group. Remember to keep the hand at a slight angle in the direction of the music. Grouping notes together for technical reasons can make the difference between a rather difficult execution and a very easy one.

The ability to play fast depends on an understanding of how to group notes. The longer the passage, the more important it is to find sub-groupings. The hand can't *conceive* of an indefinite number of notes or a long string of notes without establishing milestones along the way. If the composer writes "17" over a group of notes that are to be completed within a certain time frame, it is important to decide on how to sub-divide that group, i.e., three groups of 4 and one of five, or some other grouping that makes sense in the context. This does not mean that accents will be heard;

the group of "17" can still sound like a single unit, a flourish, if that is the desired effect. How those sub-divisions relate to the other hand is also a primary consideration. Look at Example 9-1 in chapter nine for an idea of how this works with an easy subdivision. There are 48 notes in that melisma, which comes out to four notes in the right hand for each note in the left.

Example 3-5 Chopin Ballade in G minor. Group from More Dense, the Chord.

We group from the more dense or heavier combination of notes. For example, in passages where chords are interspersed with single notes, it is much easier to feel a starting point at the chord, regardless of which part of the musical beat it comes on. In Chopin's G Minor Ballade, measure two of Example 3-5, a broken chord figure, primarily in single notes, contains a chord of a fourth placed on a weak part of the beat. By feeling a start on the chord (or a feeling of *down*), the passage immediately wants to move with ease. In my view, Chopin meant for these chords to add rhythmic interest to the passage, heightening the agitation and underscoring the seriousness of his message. Again, the thumb throws the hand over on the way down (see Figures 3-5 to 3-8) and throws the hand back on the way up.

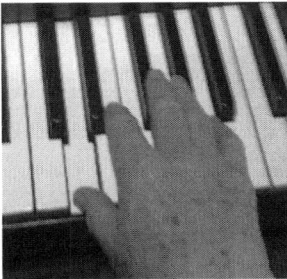

Figure 3-5 Chopin G Minor Ballade. Thumb Starts.

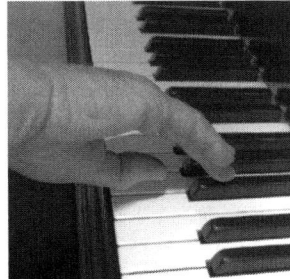

Figure 3-6 Chopin Ballade G Minor. Thumb Springs and Helps the Hand Rotate.

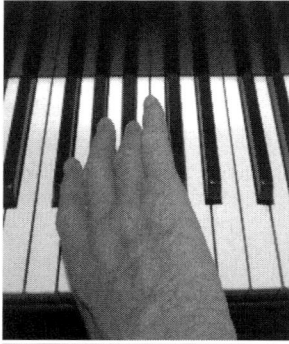

Figure 3-7 Chopin Ballade G Minor. Thumb Springs and Rotates. View from Above.

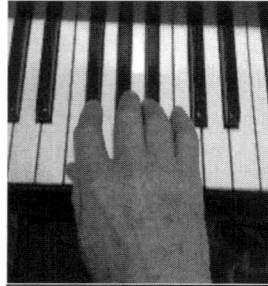

Figure 3-8 Chopin Ballade G Minor. Rotate back to New Chord.

Example 3-5 Chopin Etude Winter Wind. Grouping to Avoid Stretching.

Group notes together in order to avoid stretching the hand. In speed, it is more efficient to allow the hand to remain in a relatively closed position than it is to keep it open. That is, moving is more efficient than stretching. I know what you're thinking, it must seem counter intuitive. Just try it, and you'll feel the difference. Over long passages of quickly moving notes, if the hand remains open, with the fingers trying to do their work against that "stretch," it is possible cause strain resulting in fatigue. As always, the all-important issue is how to get from the last note of one group to the first note of the next group. In the example here,

3-5, the thumb B-flat propels the hand to five on C by means of a spring and a rotary movement. We'll have more about this in Chapter Four.

Example 3-6 Schumann Davidsbündlertänze. Group from Short to Long.

Group notes together in order to facilitate leaps with complex metric designs, i.e., short to long. The hand can't go both to and from a quick note. In general, a short note belongs technically, and probably musically as well, to the next longer note, as in dotted rhythms. In the Schumann example, 3-6, notice the leap from the end of measure two to the downbeat of measure three. The sixteenth note belongs to the next dotted quarter, so group from the thumb G.

But there are other issues at work here. Look at what we're asked to do in the first measure. The right hand plays the melody, which is on top in a dotted rhythm, *and* is required to play the offbeat part of an accompaniment pattern. Rumor has it that Schumann was not much of a pianist. Never mind, this particular chore is quite doable and is as common as holes in half notes. So, group from the chords (heavier) in both hands, leading with the left hand because it has farther to go. Here's something nice for you: Both hands then take advantage of their tendency to fall back toward the torso, returning them back to the next starting places without any noticeable effort. We use this passive movement all the time. When I practice this passage, I start on the chords and land, rotationally, on the single notes, which after playing, I allow my hands to fall back (toward the torso) and land silently on the next starting places, the chords. Piece of cake.

There are, of course, many permutations and combinations of groups and many opportunities for overlapping concepts. When you have identified groups of notes that belong together for whatever reasons, remember that the main issue is always how to get from the last note of one group to the first note of the next. What are the mechanisms that get you there? Any thoughts? Hands, please. Happy grouping.

Endnotes:

- Group for technical ease.
- The ability to play fast depends on the ability to conceive of groups of notes. The longer the passage is, the more important it is to find sub-groupings.
- Notes moving in the same direction are often grouped together.
- Group to facilitate a change of direction.
- Group to avoid stretching.
- Group from the more dense or heavier combination of notes.
- Group to facilitate leaps with complex metric designs, for example from short to long—the short note belongs to the next longer note. The hand doesn't want to go two directions at once.
- Group long, sweeping runs in order to give them an inner pulse.
- Once deciding on groupings, decide on the best means for connecting groups, i.e., rotation, shaping, walking arm, or combinations of concepts.

FOUR

ON LEAPS NEAR AND FAR

CAN I REALLY GET THERE FROM HERE?

A student came to a lesson and said, "Look how far I can stretch my hand." I thought, ouch, are we doing yoga? Then he said, "I measured it; I can reach a 10th." *Oh no*, I thought, *it's a competition*.

Well, here is a student new to my studio, a rather advanced pianist already, who suffers from a fairly common malady. Somewhere in his early studies he developed the notion that *stretching* is better than *moving*, when in fact as we've already said, the opposite is true. It is more efficient and healthier to move than it is to stretch. I know this may seem counter intuitive to some, but stay with me. I don't mean that the hand can't be open, it can, and flexible, of course. But anytime the hand is opened to an *extreme*, danger lurks in the effort. (We select fingering to avoid a stretch. See: On Fingering.)

Let me explain. If our objective is to learn how to play the piano using the body according to its design, then we must exclude efforts that act against it. Of course, many accomplished and successful musicians play the piano using various technical points of view, or more likely, no point of view at all. We wish them all the very best.

So, what are some efforts that act against the hand's design? Forcing it to open so wide that it feels tense is one. Lifting the fingers individually away from the hand, especially the fourth finger, which has tissue on top that prevents it from lifting away, is another. Yet another is angling the hands like the turnout of a ballet dancer's feet, creating a twist, which cuts off the hands from their supporting forearm. Pianists with large hands are particularly prone to this twisting in order to avoid the black keys.

Here's a useful question to ask, "What does the hand *want* to do?" It wants to be in a relatively closed position and straight with the arm. Try this: Drop your arm to the side and let it hang freely. Notice how the hand feels. This is what it wants to feel. Can we achieve this feeling in the act of playing the piano? The simple answer is *yes*, as long as we don't fall victim to suggestions in the notation that seem to be saying "stretch, pull." (See Chapter Twenty-two.)

How do we play the piano without acting against the hand, without turning it into a gnarled claw, veins bulging with tension? I'm glad you asked.

One way to use the hand according to its design is to learn how to negotiate leaps. Other issues are at work, too, underlying tools that also contribute to efficient hand use. But for now let's consider how to leap. By my definition, a leap takes place whenever the hand moves from one five-finger position to another without a thumb crossing, a shift if you like (as in string playing). It doesn't matter whether the leap is to the very next note, i.e., if you want to play stepwise with the same finger, or if you want to leap several octaves.

Here is the rule: The note *before* the leap gets us the distance. That is, the last note in the group of notes before a leap takes us to the first note of the new group by means of a springing action, like that of a diving board. It's that simple. (Well, almost.) Anxious about making a leap, pianists very often neglect to finish playing the last note of a group; they tend to skip over it. This is a pity, sometimes even tragic, because that last note is the all-important springboard for negotiating the distance to the first note of the next group. So don't be in too big a hurry.

It is just as futile to cling to that last note, losing the advantage of its thrusting power. With a well worked-in and coordinated combination of springing, *forearm rotation* and *walking arm*, leaping great distances feels like going next door. So don't be afraid to jump.

Try this. Put your index finger on your favorite key. Now, from the key, brush off an imaginary ash. Not so rough. You don't want to crush the ash. Brush it toward your torso. While doing this, imagine that there's a tread on the pad of your finger that prevents you from slipping all the way off the key. Instead, feel a downward thrust into the key, rather like flexing at the end of a diving board, which in turn provides a springing reaction upward. This is the tricky part. Let go. Yes, allow your arm to become a dead weight in the air and allow it—don't place it—to drop into your lap. This is how we use the rebound action of the key to help us move laterally without an active movement. This rebound is passive, and gravity, if we let it, will assist us. Physics again. And physics was my least favorite class in high school because the teacher spent six weeks talking about weather, and in Southern California in those days we didn't have weather.

Next, once you have really felt what it's like to let the key send your arm into the air and become a dead weight, try allowing it with an active finger, to land on your next favorite key, or perhaps your same favorite key an octave or two higher. See Figure 4-4 for a view of the arc described by the hand. Notice that the highest point is over the landing spot. Speaking of which, as you prepare to spring from that diving board, be sure to see if there's water in the pool, that is, notice where you want to land.

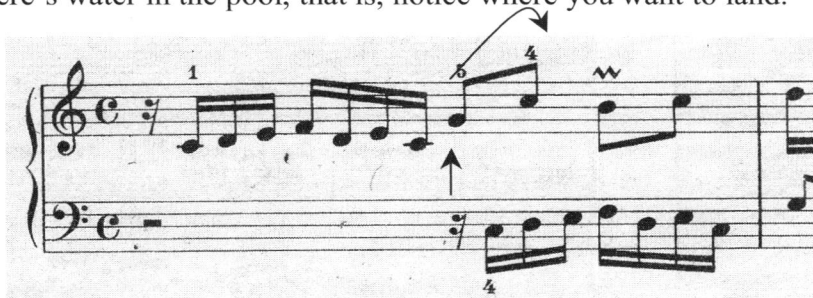

Example 4-1 Bach Invention No. 1 Leaping

Figure 4-1 Bach Invention No. 1 Leaping. Spring from G and Rotate.

Figure 4-2 Bach Invention No. 1 Leaping. High Point Over Landing Note.

If we want to use the fingering suggested by the editor in the above example, 4-1, we must get the hand from a five-finger position on C (fifth finger on G) to a new five-finger position on G (fourth finger on C). A shift in hand position requires some form of

Figure 4-3 Bach Invention No. 1 Leaping. Rotating Back to 4th Finger, Dropping into Key.

locomotion for getting the distance. In this case, spring from the G (5), which when combined with the lateral walking arm, gets us the distance to a place over the C (4), after which the hand rotates into position and drops down into the key. Notice that the high point is over the landing place, not somewhere equidistant between the two notes (Figure 4-4).

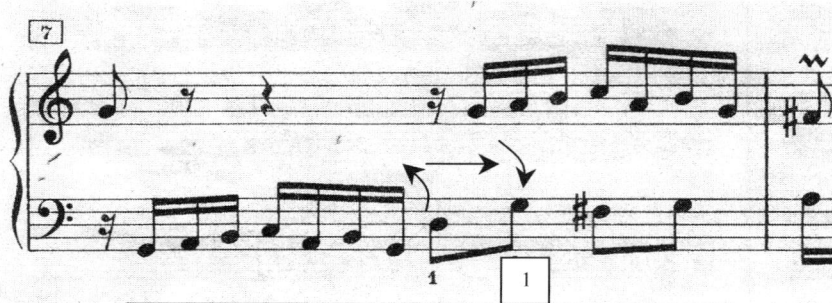

Example 4-2 Bach Invention No. 1 Leaping. Thumb to Thumb.

What if in the above example, 4-2, I wanted to use the thumb where the editor has indicated second finger? Just for instance. Now that we know about rotation, springing and the walking arm, it is quite easy to play two thumbs in a row. Once

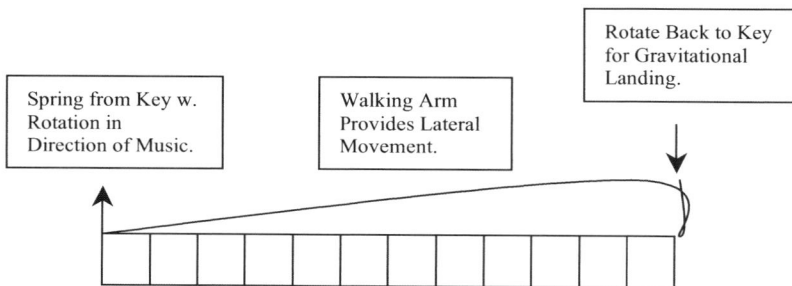

Figure 4-4 View of Keys from Front.

you try this you won't want to stop. The thumb springs and rotates away from D. The arm then walks the hand to its new position over the G and rotates down into the key. In both of these Bach examples, the leap helps articulate the sub-phrases, thus helping us make a musical choice. I love it when the music and the technique communicate.

The Bach Invention was just a warm-up. We have lots more leaping to do. Look again at Example 3-6 from the previous chapter. We grouped the left hand in pairs of eighths starting with the chord, the principle being that we group from heavier to lighter. This is also a leap from top to bottom, from the chord to the single note. Here, we spring from the chord and using a walking arm, land on the single note. Then we allow the hand to fall back to the next starting place. Remember that the hands fall naturally toward the torso.

Now comes the really neat part. Remember that rounded keyboard, the one that never caught on? It didn't catch on, I'm quite sure, because our clever bodies realized we didn't need it. Pay close attention: The arm and hand act as a single unit hinged at the elbow, which swings laterally. Try it now. Don't allow your upper arm to move outward, only swing from the elbow. If you look at your hand while doing this, you'll notice it describes an arc, which is probably what gave the inventor of that ill-fated instrument the idea. The reason we don't need that circular keyboard is that we can use this arc-like movement to our advantage as long as we remain straight with ourselves. It's quite okay to be at an angle with the keyboard. So, the principle here is that we group these leaps in pairs, using a passive rebound, in order to avoid making the arm feel that it's trying to go two directions at once. Trying to move back and forth at the same time can cause a jam. I call it lockjaw of the arm. This is not nice. A word of caution again: Always notice where you want to land before you start to leap.

Example 4-3 Chopin Ballade G Minor. Leaps. Coordinate w. Left and Right.

In the Chopin example above, 4-3, the composer gives us a left hand passage similar to the one in Schumann. This time, though, the leap is from a single note, second finger B-flat, to another single note. The mechanism is the same. Spring, rotate, walk and fall back to the next starting point. Notice that the grouping is again from the heavy to the light. Take care to move your torso slightly to the right in order to avoid a crash into your side, which might result in a twist in your hand. We don't like to leap into a twist, so get out of your way.

This passage is interesting for other reasons. Can you see that the right hand plays rotationally for the first five beats? Now look at the second quarter in both hands. Chopin puts a heavier group of notes, a chord, on a relatively weak beat. At the same time he dramatically changes direction in the right hand, starting a downward trend after leaping upward to that second beat. So, feel a starting place, hands together, on the second beat and again on the fifth beat. This makes the technical organization feel quite easy. It isn't necessary to make accents at these technical starting places. Feel the groupings without necessarily hearing them. This is what we mean we say that the technique is at the service of the music and not the other way around. We don't want to be at the mercy of our technique, making musical choices because of technical inadequacy.

Example 4-4 Chopin Ballade G Minor.
Leaps. Coordination Between Hands.

Above (Example 4-4) is the beginning of the fearsome coda in the G minor ballade. Don't be frightened. All you have to do (almost) is remember to group from heavier to lighter. So, the right hand plays down on the second beat and—look at that—the composer gives us an accent. Then the left hand plays down on the third beat. If we scan the passage, it looks like the two hands alternate downs. Right is down on beat two, left hand is down on beat three, and so on. The arrows in the example indicate down-up. The left hand is about leaping, as we've described before: Spring from the chord to the single note and fall back to the new chord. The right hand is more about feeling down on the chord and a slight up on the single note, more of a grouping issue, though there is a slight shape *in* to the black key.

Now try this. Tap down on your desk top, alternating first right then left hands. It's like marching: Right-left-right-left. (Notice how I'm not mentioning my army drill sergeant, who didn't know his left from his right.) Now try this at the piano. Start from the third beat left-hand chord with down. Now here's the trick: While the left hand comes up on the fourth beat, the right hand goes down. I know. It's a little like patting your head and rubbing your stomach. But you can do that, right?

Now we're ready for dessert. Look at measure three. The left hand continues its down up leaping motion while the right hand has a group of four eighths, starting with a heavy chord. If you think of starting on this beat, the second beat, with right hand down while the left hand comes up, well, it's a piece of cake. Have it now.

FIVE

ON PRACTICING

HOW SLOW?

If you've been studying the preceding chapters carefully, then you may be ready for a break. There's a method to my digression, though, because practicing is how we teach technical concepts to our hands. As you will discover, *practicing* is always conscious, deliberate and anything but mindless rote.

I want to explain here, at the out set, the purpose of slow practice, a concept of which we all have heard a great deal. This is the cipher of the piano teacher. One hears it in the wind, in the very walls of our practice rooms. But what does it mean and why do we do it? First, the why: Since in our study here we are learning specific movements that propel us efficiently from one note to the next, we have something to actually practice. Ah, I used the word *practice*. By *practice* I really mean *repeat* or *work-in*. That is, once we have identified a particular solution to a problem, a certain movement, we can then repeat it under tempo. We now have the ability to use at a slow tempo what we need for speed. Let that sink in. In slow practice we should be using what we need in speed. The failure of many students who mean well by practicing slowly is that when they play slowly, they do something different from what is required in speed. Then they wonder why it doesn't work in speed. Imagine.

There are three main types of practicing, and many variables. The first type of practicing we employ in learning a *new piece* (or a new technical concept). The second type is for a piece that is *in progress*; the third type is for a *finished piece*, one that is ready or nearly ready for performance. In an ideal world, there will be fewer *new pieces* at any given time than *in-progress* or *finished pieces*. All practice requires intense focus and concentration. But I find that the concentration required in the solving of problems in a new piece can be the most intense and should therefore come at the beginning of the practice session, when the mind is fresh.

Psychological impediments sometimes stand in the way of good practicing, or of even getting started. Have you ever caught yourself thinking, as you fondly eye your piano, well I'd better start the laundry first, or check the mail? Or is there a sinister voice lurking deep within that is ever so eager to point out that it's really too difficult and everyone else is better anyway, so why even bother? I call these psychological impediments the *committee*. It sits on our shoulders giving negative feedback. "Just sit down whether you want to or not," says cellist Gordon Epperson. And he's right. The ritual of preparing to work itself can be cathartic.

But there's more to it than that, of course. While getting set up, think about a basic plan, i.e., what types of pieces will you practice: *new, in progress, finished*. Where will you start and what is the first thing you will do and how will you do it? In other words, *think first* before the hand touches the keys. It is the thinking process that protects us from falling victim to what I call *mindless rote*, which is when automatic pilot takes over from the deliberate act of thinking about what you are doing. If you find yourself thinking about what's for lunch, take a break. Take a short walk, go for a coffee, read a chapter, play solitaire (but don't wear out your thumbs texting). For most types of practicing, one hour at a time with a 10 or 15-minute break between hours is ideal. At the end of the break start the *thinking* over again: where will I start, what will I do and how will I do it---*where, what, how*?

THE PLAN

NEW PIECE

1. *Scan*. Play through the piece at a comfortable tempo, stopping and starting as necessary, not to amaze yourself with what a fine sight-reader you are, but rather to identify problem spots. *Mark the hard spots.*
2. *Focus*. Having located spots that need extra attention, figure out possible fingerings, several even. *Write these in the music* in pencil. You won't remember them, I promise. When deciding on fingerings, try to keep the musical intentions of the composer in mind. (See "Fingering Concepts.")
3. *Limit*. Reduce the amount of information you process, even down to just one interval or one leap. Start this very slowly and *gradually*, increasing the tempo to as close to the performance tempo as you can, but not faster than you can at this early point. If you detect a hand coordination issue, try each hand separately, but only in that spot, not for the entire piece. Hands separately is too time consuming and

counter productive to practice for the entire piece. Remember, if there's a coordination issue, it usually means that one hand is trying to do what the other is doing. Check the rotation in each hand. Then compare those movements by trying hands together.

4. *Proceed.* Go on to the next hard spot. Do not try to put the measures together yet. Make notes in the margin if you have questions about technical or musical issues. Do this very detailed work for as long as you can concentrate fully. (This type of practice has a learning curve, but in the long run it will cut your required practice time for a successful performance by at least 50%, probably more.)

5. *Context.* Once a particular spot is feeling *easy* and rather consistent, even if not quite up to tempo, try putting it in context with the material immediately before it and immediately after. Do this several times. *Do not force the tempo.* A good technique is one that feels easy, never rushed, even in speed.

6. *Tempo.* Hard spots must be worked up through several tempos from very slow to the performance tempo. When you're ready to work up the tempo, that is, when you have solved the technical problem(s), remember to play *No slower than you need to and no faster than you can.* The metronome can be useful here to keep track of your progress.

7. *Music.* The objective, always, is to make music. Keep in mind the quality of sound, the type of articulation required for the musical effect, the dynamic variety.

A PIECE IN PROGRESS

1. *Evaluate.* Make conscious decisions as to what sections need the most technical work. Start with those sections, working through several tempos. Most work should be under performance tempo. Keep in mind that the technique should always feel easy and unhurried.

2. *Perform.* Try playing at tempo or near tempo in *phrases* or *musical sections.* For example, look at the musical form and select part of a section such as a first theme group or the development or the "A" section. This is also a good tool for examining the overall structure or architecture of the

piece. Do not play through the piece non-stop at this point.

3. *Shapes*. Look for musical shapes. Where are the highest points in pitch? The lowest? What direction does a line seem to move over all? One approach to bringing the music to life is to play with increasing intensity as a line moves up and less intensity as a line moves down. This is just a starting point, of course.

4. *Articulation*. The length of individual notes has a great deal to do with musical expression. Should a group of notes be played very short or played with exaggerated length? What combinations of notes can be grouped under the hand without a thumb crossing? The composer or editor often makes these decisions, but they are not cut in stone. If I'm certain that the articulation is from the composer, then I make every effort to oblige. Fingerings, though, even if from Beethoven himself, should be honored with a glace and accepted or rejected with impunity.

5. *Dynamics*. Make some clear choices about how loud or soft a given passage will be. Where is the loudest place in the piece? The softest? Where are the crescendos? Are any passages especially accented?

FINISHED PIECE

1. *Musical Objective*. As you worked through the previous section, particularly on *shapes, articulation* and *dynamics*, you will have begun to form opinions about the meaning of the music. Ask yourself what the piece is about (happy? sad?). What is it that you like about it? How will you make your listener hear what you hear?

2. *Practice Performing Sections*. At this point it is time to start playing in large sections, i.e., an entire exposition or from point A to point B, without stopping. Try to incorporate everything that you have considered in the above. Don't be discouraged if it doesn't come off as planned on the first try. Keep in mind that the technique should always feel easy, unforced, unhurried.

3. *Practice Performing*. Play the entire piece through up to tempo without stopping no matter what happens. This is a diagnostic tool and sometimes it can be helpful to record the effort. Afterward, consider how close you came to

meeting your goals. It won't be 100% the first time. Don't expect it to be. Do whatever cleanup is necessary. Make notes in the score. Try again, but not more than 3 times in one sitting. After the final try, do whatever cleanup you need, i.e., slow technical work. Then *leave it*. Go on to something else or take a break.

4. *Practice Performing Slowly.* Play the entire piece as a performance, but well under tempo. This removes much of the tactile memory, requiring more thoughtful, deliberate playing. It is also a very good test of memory

Ninety percent of practicing is slower than performance tempo.

A student once wrote to me as follows: "So I play every single day, at least 3 hours and some of the time feel like I am in control of my playing completely, while other days I feel like I never played piano."

Well, everyone has a bad day occasionally. But what this student describes probably has as much to do with focus at that particular moment as with preparation. But I suspect the quality of his practicing is deficient in some way. This is a valid subject to bring up with a teacher. How should I practice? What should I do with a given passage?

As I point out above, most practicing is under tempo and in small segments. In this way details are more easily absorbed. I begin with the most problematic spots; I almost never begin at the first measure (unless that's a problem spot). Then, there is "performance" practicing, in which I play through without stopping and then take stock of how it sounded and how it felt.

A lesson, for me, is not necessarily a performance in which the student plays through a piece. I would rather the student show me the places where he/she has trouble, rather than try to hide problems (as one does in a performance). We can then work on the problems together.

Ideally, the working-out process protects us from making errors. If we first decide on technical solutions (fingerings, shapes, what the hand needs) and then work these solutions in gradually from slow to fast (not slower than you need or faster than you can), then the learning process is always positive. I point out that a learning process is always taking place whether it's right or wrong. So, it behooves us to practice thoughtfully and with deliberation.

Avoid rote playing at all costs. So, *the working-out* comes first—the figuring out of solutions, technical and musical. The *working-in* is the process of establishing physical habits that will carry us though in performance.

SIX

ON MEMORIZING

BUT IS THIS REALLY NECESSARY?

A student who reads quite well but had been having trouble memorizing her music asked about a plan for memorizing. So often, students rely on mindless repetition to somehow hammer the music into their brains by striking the piano with their fingers as firmly as possible. Well, we already know that this is not the way to technical mastery, and I'm prepared to tell you that it is not the way to reliable memorization. Trying to teach only the fingers is like telling a child not to touch fire, without telling her why not. In performance, of course, we rely on automatic responses. But if we don't explain to our fingers why they are playing the notes they play, relying only on digital memory, the other memory tools—the aural, visual and intellectual—won't be associated with those notes. I can't tell you how many times I've passed practice rooms and heard the angry hammering of a single note, which I suppose is somehow meant to secure that particular note in the memory. Or maybe it's to punish the piano for messing up.

Here's a basic plan. Once you've tried it, you can adjust it to suit your own needs.

- Make a conscious decision to memorize. *Accidental* memorizing is usually muscle memory primarily and this is not totally reliable.
- Select a small amount of music to consider. This could be the first measure or the first phrase. It could also be a particularly complicated passage in the middle of the piece.
- Look at the example and notice whatever you can about it, i.e., there is a broken chord figure; there is a scale figure; the R.H is the same as (or different from) the L.H; one hand leaps while the other stays put; one hand makes a leap but to the same note 2 octaves higher. I even say these things out loud. (My cats seem to enjoy that.)
- Play the example from the score very slowly.
- Look away from the score and play as much as you can, still very slowly. Repeat this process until you can play that example reliably, still very slowly and deliberately. The

slow, deliberate playing will help you engage the other types of memory: aural, visual, intellectual, minimizing the digital.

- Move on to the next section and repeat the process. Do not try to connect the two sections yet.

When you can't concentrate anymore, stop. At the next practice session continue where you left off. When you have finished the new material for the day, then go back and review the old material, one section at a time, or if it feels right, try playing two sections together. You may need to refer to the score again; this is normal. But you can tell yourself that you know this material.

Once you have learned the piece and have it up to tempo, practice playing the entire piece excruciatingly slowly. This takes away much of the digital memory and will help you locate places that are fuzzy. It is also a useful test, though more difficult, to practice away from the piano. Close your eyes and see your hands on the keys, playing the piece very slowly, thinking of each note in advance of playing it. This is what I call playing on purpose, playing deliberately.

If in trying out a performance from memory a slip occurs, keep in mind that very often a so-called memory slip is no such thing. In fact I would venture to say that in most cases such a slip has more to do with the working-in of technique than it does with forgetting the music. Try this. If a slip occurs, revisit the decisions you made about that place in the score and see if you might have missed something relating to the physicality of the passage. Of course, slow passages can often be the most difficult to recall because muscle memory is not a leading factor. This is why it is important to practice these sections on purpose, deliberately, one beat at a time, in order to engage the aural, visual and intellectual capacities. While doing this, take pains to attach as much meaning as you can to each iteration of sound and how it relates to preceding and succeeding sounds. What are the dynamics, the articulations? How have you planned the voicing? What is the passage about?

Having said all that, I feel moved to offer the following. Playing without the score is (ought to be) a matter of personal choice. Some feel using the score frees them to make music, though others feel the score is an impediment. Most musicians who are non-pianists are permitted to appear on stage fully clothed, as it were, without so much as a raised eyebrow. As of this writing in the second decade of the twenty-first century, the performance standard is still somewhat discriminatory against pianists, though not as much as in the previous century. For competitions, yes, don't even think of trying to show up with a score. But in actual concert halls one occasionally hears celebrated artists perform with the score.

This of course is not new. In Beethoven's time it was the norm to play with the score. He reportedly chastised mightily his student Carl Czerny who dared present with a memorized sonata. The master felt that all the markings he had been so particular about when composing his sonata would be lost during feats of memory. And Chopin wasn't at all happy when one of his students intended to perform a nocturne off-book. This, he felt, trivialized the music. The audience might think the music was being improvised on the spot and not take it seriously.

There are famous precedents that date from the nineteenth century, the century in which Liszt (or Clara Schumann, take your pick) decided to add a bit more show to their performances and fly without a net. I like to think it was Clara who bucked tradition—it had been there-to-fore considered the height of impudence and presumption to play someone else's music without the score. My personal view is that Clara, a woman on a man's concert stage, decided to make her appearances a little more sensational. I don't know if that's true, but it would have been an excellent marketing strategy. She did have a unique and highly successful career as a performing artist, forging a trail not only for women but establishing what we know of today as the piano recital.

We know from Clara's letters that as she became a forty-something she felt less secure without the score and began using it. She does deserve a break, though. She suffered through ten pregnancies and bore eight children, was wife to the famous composer, Robert, championing his music in her concerts, composed many fine compositions and traveled Europe every season performing. And she wrote letters almost daily. We have thousands of them. There is an anecdote from Mendelssohn, a friend of the Schumann's, who expressed to Clara his appreciation for the degree to which she enjoyed his spinning song, as she made so many repetitions not indicated in the score. Perhaps it was this memory lapse that persuaded her to take up the score for performances.

In the twentieth century, Myra Hess famously replied to a reporter asking about her use of the score in concert: "The band has theirs. Why shouldn't I have mine?" Sviatoslov Richter used the score later in his career, explaining that something about a change in his sense of pitch made it necessary. He also preferred subtle stage lighting and smaller halls. It sounds like nerves to me. But he was one of the greats.

I've had the privilege of hearing in concert many of the greatest pianists of the twentieth century, and can report that almost no one is immune from a slip now and again. If this causes unease in the audience, who can then no longer enjoy the music for fear of a disaster, then I say what a pity memorization has become between the artist and the listener.

But, as a tool for understanding the music inside and out, memorization is an excellent way to work. You can decide for yourself if you do better on stage with or without the score. Whatever you do, don't sight-read concerts as one famous pianist reportedly did early in his career.

SEVEN

ON PERFORMANCE ANXIETY

Have you ever wondered why a performance might sometimes go very well in the practice room or your living room, but not so well with an audience present? If we work out the technical and musical details and if we drill repeatedly in order to secure memory, why then isn't a successful performance always a sure thing? Well, to paraphrase the Gershwins, performance is a sometime thing. True, perhaps, but it ain't necessarily so, not always.

We are all familiar with performance variables. There is a strange piano in a strange room. Now there are people, where before there were none. There are stage lights, hot and bright. Perhaps we didn't sleep well the night before or weren't able to rest during the afternoon of the performance. I could go on and on. Every performer has some sort of ritual upon which they hang success. Students, too, playing perhaps only for their teacher or for a jury exam, experience similar variables. What, I ask, do all of these variables have in common? Focusing on them distracts us from our work.

All performers—great and small, student or seasoned artist—experience performance anxiety. Some call it *butterflies.* I call it *the committee.* This committee sits on my shoulders, explaining to me that I have no business on the stage, that anyone else could do a better job. They whisper in my ear irrelevant details, just to distract me from the work at hand. *You should have checked that passage again. This is a huge program and you haven't even started yet. Last week "il grande pianista" played here on this very stage. You're ugly and your mother dresses you funny...*

I once worked with a very successful soprano who explained to me that the possibility of failure never occurred to her, that for her the stage is where she comes to life. She was indeed very confident and I think in all the years I performed with her, she missed perhaps one word. But even she experienced jitters before going out on stage. For her though, the jitters seemed to be a combination of the excitement of the performance about to take place and the need to get out there and do it, like a stallion champing at the bit. There was a violinist in my stable of artists who had a similar temperament. She explained to me that it was being in the audience that she found more disagreeable; she would rather be on the stage performing.

These two artists I place at the extreme end of the performance personality spectrum, the end where confidence resides. They both seem to be as close to *natural* performers as it is possible to be. They crave the limelight and thrive in its glow with very little second-guessing of their abilities. It's the second-guessing that gets stuck in the craw of those closer to the opposite end of the performance personality spectrum. This, I think, is at the root of the problem of anxiety.

There is nothing quite like knowing exactly how you do what it is you intend to do in order to instill confidence. Elsewhere in this volume I refer to a quote attributed to the great pianist Vladimir Horowitz, who refused invitations to teach because he felt he didn't know how he did it. Do we think, perhaps, that this feeling contributed to his reported breakdown and his absence for more than a decade from the concert stage? Possibly. I can say for sure, though, that in my case, understanding the mechanisms I employ when performing make an enormous difference in my attitude and demeanor before and during concerts. Even if something doesn't go as planned, it is comforting to know why it didn't go as planned and what to do in order to fix it. I should pause here to point out that, despite the slight titillation I get from referring to myself alongside Horowitz, I do not make any comparisons with this dynamic artist and yours truly.

Imagine for a moment that you are standing at the top of a high diving board. You have been asked to perform a swan dive. Glancing around, you notice all eyes on you. Cleverly, you take the trouble to notice whether there is any water in the pool. Then, you suddenly realize you don't know how to do a swan dive and that you've never been so high before. Actually, you don't even know how to swim. This could be anxiety provoking. My mother used to tell a story from her youth about swinging high over a lake, just to enjoy the view, or so she claimed. She didn't say, but I expect she was showing off for the gentlemen down below. Suddenly, as the swing pulled to its highest point, she slipped off and, according to witnesses, performed a perfect swan dive into the lake. Yes, she could swim. "Do it again, Betty," they demanded. "No, I don't feel like it right now," she replied, and I can see her patting her head and slipping away to catch her breath.

We are talking here about a happy accident. Please note, though, that there is a difference between the happy accident and a planned enterprise. If we neglect our advance preparation, hoping things will somehow turn out well, chances are the nerves will not survive.

So, you may be wondering, what are the mechanisms I employ when performing? Can you guess? Yes, we've already covered many of them, but taken as a group, let's call them the *demystification of technique*. If we know how to produce clearly articulated scales, secure leaps, fast and accurate octaves and all of the other technical demands in the repertoire we play, we are entitled—yes, I mean entitled—to say to ourselves, to our committees, that we know the music, we know how to produce on demand what is required. We can give ourselves permission to perform. It's this permission that, for me, helps to silence the committee. That is, when we walk out on stage we need to have a good conscience, the feeling that everything has been done that can be done to ensure a fine performance; we shouldn't judge ourselves during the playing— the *post mortem* comes afterward; we should focus and concentrate on the specific issues at hand, staying in the moment. With experience, the mind can be trained to filter out negative voices by replacing them with positive actions.

Once when I was an undergraduate, I was invited to perform a short modern piece on a television program hosted by my teacher. It was to be filmed live and there would be no opportunity for retakes. Already the anxiety begins to rise. I played reasonably well, I thought, though during my *post mortem* I concluded that one tricky passage wasn't really clear. When I viewed the broadcast, though, the passage sounded clear and well articulated, contradicting my recollection. So here's something to remember: The body communicates to the brain what it is experiencing during performance. The brain may get the message that something didn't *sound* right because it didn't *feel* right physically. So it doesn't help to dwell on this in the performance. Our conclusions, then, are these: Wait until after the performance to evaluate how it went and take care to prepare well in advance every passage using your specific knowledge of how to solve the technical problems.

When is a memory slip not a memory slip? Playing from memory can be anxiety inducing. If ever you've suffered a so-called *memory slip* on or off stage, you know that the possibility exists and the fear of a repeat can be debilitating. What if I said a memory slip is often not about memory at all? That's right. There's probably nothing wrong with your memory. It is more likely that there is some defect in your working out of the physical movements involved. That is, you may not have completely solved the technical requirements or completely worked them into motor memory, upon which we rely in speed. Slow passages elude us perhaps more often than quick ones. Any guesses as to why? That's right we can't rely on digital memory in very slow passages. This makes it all the more imperative that we engage the other types of memory, aural, visual and intellectual. In slower passages, the musical idea becomes our most important tool. (See Chapter Six on memorizing.)

So far, we've been discussing preparation. Careful, deliberate working in of technical solutions produces the necessary confidence to perform. What do we take with us onto the stage? What do we take besides the confidence that knowledge brings? Here are some steps to try.

1. Find a still point in your mind. I call this a safe house.
2. Focus on the breath. Take regular, slow breaths. This will slow the pulse and increase the chances that your tempos will be accurate and not too fast.
3. Think about the piece you are about to play. Have this in your mind when you walk out onto the stage, even while bowing. This will help to draw the audience to you and prevent the audience from drawing you to them. That is, your focus—your concentration—will draw them to you. This, after all, is why they came to the concert. They want to hear the music you produce.
4. Finally, and most important of all, take with you the idea of the music. Imagine that you are telling a story with colorful characters, places and events. This you've worked out before hand, but take the general concept with you onto the stage and as you begin, set the first scene and the rest will fall into place.

Do these points seem somewhat romanticized and perhaps easier said than done? There is a story about the distinguished harpsichordist Wanda Landowska, an artist celebrated as the medium through whom Bach spoke with regularity. An earnest young reporter, who was clearly awestruck by Madame Landowska's ability to commune with the gods, once asked her what she thought about when performing. The formidable woman raised her eyebrows and replied, "The notes, dear, the notes."

EIGHT

ON LEGATO *AT THE PIANO*

IS THERE AN ILLUSIONIST IN THE HOUSE?

In a discussion on *legato*, a contributor to an online forum opined that she didn't accept the notion that the piano is a percussive instrument. This is like not accepting the notion that the earth is round. I have my faults, certainly, but I've learned to accept and deal with the laws of physics. When my head stopped spinning I thought to myself, well, she is probably lost in that world where we artistic types often go, the world of wishful thinking. I responded: "My piano has hammers that strike strings. What does your piano have?" I heard back: "Good point. My piano has a choir inside, with an organ to accompany it. Sounds like yours has a wrecking crew. What the heck, to each his own." This was quite a funny response, I thought, and food for thought.

That writer has identified the place where opinion and fact collide. Or to put it in more useful terms, where imagery and practice coexist. On the one hand, imagery is great. It can help us to conceptualize a desired result and for some pianists, some of the time, that may be enough. But, if it isn't enough, what then? For me, knowledge wins out over fancy; I want to know how.

Legato on the piano is an illusion at best because the piano is a percussive instrument. It does have hammers that strike strings no matter how much you would rather it were home to an organ and a choir. But imagine the upkeep. (Personally, I would take the string section from the Philadelphia Orchestra, but who could pay all those salaries.) Some of the advice offered in the forum discussion was right on the money, i.e., a finger *legato* is about over-holding until the next note is depressed. There is another important factor, though, and that is how the finger connects with the key. For a finger *legato* always play from the key, not from above the key. This cushions the attack and makes the connections seem more *legato*. A physicist will tell you that quality is determined by the number and prominence of overtones, and because of that fact, the faster you strike the key, the more the upper and more dissonant partials vibrate, making an even more percussive sound. Isn't physics a great science?

Consider playing succeeding notes in or under the decay of the preceding note. This will give a very nice simulation of *legato*; it also implies a *diminuendo*, which may not be called for. In any case, take care to consider where in the phrase hierarchy each succeeding note belongs. After a long melodic note, for example, listen well to how the phrase continues. Does the phrase require a new impetus? Or should it sound like a continuation of the long note? Is the phrase rising dynamically or falling? Music is not a democracy; not every note gets an equal vote.

Finally, perhaps more importantly, it's the *legato* pedal, sometimes referred to as *syncopated* pedal that needs particular attention. The pedal gives us the ability to over-hold a particular note while moving away from it, thus creating a sense of *legato*. The way in which the key is depressed is still important. With the pedal down, strike the next note with just enough weight to override the reverberating sound, to give the illusion of connectedness, the new note floating above the din.

Another contributor to the forum remarked haphazardly that everyone plays *legato* all the time and it isn't necessary to practice it particularly. He maintained, "If it isn't *legato*, it's *staccato*." At first I opted to let this go as, well, sloppy thinking, but it began to eat away at me.

Does everyone play *legato* all the time, even in Czerny studies (shudder), as he says? We know that up to Mozart's time the default articulation was detached, changing with Beethoven, who reportedly quipped that "Mozart's playing sounded like so many chickens dancing on the keys." Since Beethoven's time pianists have worked to develop a singing style, a *legato* touch. I think here the operative word is *worked*. I decided that arbitrarily putting one finger down after another thoughtlessly wouldn't necessarily produce the illusion of *legato*. It's important to consider the above, over-holding slightly, the manner of attack, i.e., from the key, not from above, where the note comes in the musical hierarchy of the phrase and how to use the pedal. When imagery isn't sufficient, we can arm ourselves with the laws of physics and bring that world of wishful thinking closer to a musical reality.

NINE

ON FINGERING

CONCEPTS THAT GOVERN CHOICES

A student came to me recently and asked how to finger a certain passage, claiming that the editor's fingering didn't feel right. This is often the case with editions and you can tell a lot about someone's understanding of technique when looking at their fingerings. I've often thought that some of these editors must have put in their fingerings while riding the bus on the way to their day jobs.

My student's question was fair enough, as all questions are, so I set about writing in a fingering for him. I explained as I went what sort of physical movement the passage required, which was the rationale for the fingering I set down. Then it occurred to me to play the devil's advocate and show him some other possibilities based on a different technical approach. (I wouldn't try this with a less advanced pianist.) When he tried the various solutions I offered, his response was a very satisfactory, "Wow, this one feels so much easier than that one." I allowed as how that was the correct response.

Here are some thoughts, then, on how to choose fingering. These concepts are not original to me; they have been in the pianistic consciousness for about as long as there have been pianos. I learned them from Dorothy Taubman, who takes credit for organizing them, not inventing them, and Edna Golandsky, who brilliantly illustrated them. Over the years, though, they have become mine, refined and shaped as I applied them to my own playing and teaching.

You'll notice that nowhere in this discussion is a mention of hand size. So here are a few words about that. Hand size is almost irrelevant; every hand has the same number of fingers and physical properties that mechanize those fingers. Yes, pianists with thicker fingers have to make adjustments when called upon to play in the black keys. Yes, pianists with longer fingers have to make adjustments in order not to twist when avoiding the black keys. And yes, a person with a wider hand has an advantage when it comes to large filled-in chords, especially octaves with a minor third between thumb and first finger. But if underlying principles of movement are well understood, the progression of the fingers up and down the keyboard, that is, the walking from note to note, is virtually the same in every hand.

That the hand falls most naturally onto the keys with the long fingers on short keys, short fingers on long keys we have already discovered. Also, we know that the hand is most comfortable in its closed position. It probably doesn't take a pianist to suppose either of these two propositions. We know, too, that the position of the thumb when passing under the hand is approximately behind the finger that is playing and that it shouldn't feel pulled or held under or against the hand. It plays rotationally. The hand remains straight with the arm, but may be at an angle with the keyboard, not twisted, i.e., to avoid the black keys. All of this we know, but I recap it here because it forms a backdrop for our discussion.

Let's consider now the much-maligned fourth finger. How many times have you been told—or thought—that the fourth finger is weak? Wait while I count the hands. Yes, that's everyone. I have to admit that it does seem weak if I try to lift it away from the hand. But this is not the sort of movement that it was designed to do, so it seems unreasonable to ask that of it. There is tissue preventing the finger from lifting away from the hand, which should tell us, if we're listening, not to do that. Here's the good news: The fourth finger can be made to feel and sound as strong as the others if it is allowed to drop downward into the key. How is this accomplished? Yes that's right, by making use of principles we've already discussed, forearm rotation, shaping, walking arm. In fact, all of our digits can sound strong and they can articulate independently of one another, but only if they act as part of a whole. Have you heard the expression *independence of fingers*? Many of the well-meaning studies we come across in our pianistic lives claim to train for this, when in fact, if one does what these studies seem to ask, only discomfort and fatigue will result. The fingers are not independent agents, but they can be made to sound that way.

Look again at Example 2-2, Mozart K. 333, first movement. Notice that the fourth and fifth fingers play in a quick passage demanding clarity and precision. The distribution of the notes in the passage puts the fourth and fifth fingers at a disadvantage, lying as they do on the outside of the hand through no fault of their own. If they are asked to play as separate units, they will balk. But, if they are allowed to play as part of a shape that puts the support of the forearm behind them, they will sing clearly and firmly and they and your audience will thank you for the consideration.

Let's break a taboo: The thumb and fifth fingers may play on the black keys. Yikes. How do we do that? Well, the answer is with ease, as long as it is understood how to get there and away again. When we discovered the *in-out* shape, we realized that the short fingers, one and five, bring the hand in when played on the black keys. The question, then, is how do we get from *out* when playing with short fingers on the white keys to *in* when using them on black keys? One way is to walk gradually, one key at a time, toward the required black key in order to arrive there just in time to play. Do not wait until the last note before the black key and then make a sudden lurch *in*. This can cause a ripple in both the sound and in the feel of the passage. This walking-in idea is cousin to what other concept? That's right, shaping.

Speaking of taboos, consider this: Despite what you may have heard, the fifth finger may cross over the thumb and the thumb may cross over the fifth finger, particularly in the playing of dominant seventh arpeggios. But I do this whenever convenient, now that I know how. Have a look at the end of this melisma of 48 notes in Example 9-1 below. Notice the editor's fingering at the high point turn around, from F and descending. Try the 1-4-3-2-1 combination as shown in the example with an added slur line. When I first played this as a teenager, not knowing any better, this is the fingering I used. Very uncomfortable and not really fluent. Now try 1-3-2-1-5 on the same group of notes and continue as marked in the top fingering. The thumb is the mechanism by which the hand moves rotationally from one on D-flat to five on a white key, C-flat. Yes, cross five over one, one being the thrusting agent.

Example 9-1 Chopin Nocturne Op. 27, No. 2. Fingering. Five Over One.

Example 9-2 Beethoven Appassionata, 3rd Movmt. Fingering.

The inside row of fingering in Example 9-2 is one I've used for many years and every time I take up this movement, I have to remind myself not to play too fast. That's how easy it is. So, play on the black keys or move to and from the black keys with long or short fingers at will. Just be aware of how and when to get there.

We know that piano keys are levers, so the point of least resistance is at the end farthest from the fulcrum. We can conclude, therefore, that the thumb should not be required to hang above the white keys, which forces the long fingers to play farther in. The thumb may be off the keyboard entirely until it is needed, and when it is needed, because it is a short appendage, it likes to play in the *direction of in.* That is, the thumb plays toward the fallboard, but not necessarily in among the black keys.

We hold these truths to be self evident, that fingering is selected to avoid stretching, so we use a thumb crossing instead. We select fingering to avoid crowding, i.e., thumb next to 5. We know that arbitrarily avoiding 5-5 or 1-1 is not necessary and select fingering accordingly to suit our convenience. Choosing consistent fingering merely because the shape of a passage is consistent (i.e., as in a sequence) is not necessary. We are hereby and forevermore granted permission to uncross hands where feasible if we want to. Now that we understand about forearm rotation, we don't need to arbitrarily change fingers on repeated notes because it is not necessary. Remember those old wives? The preceding is a particularly egregious example of their legacy.

And now a word about score reading as it pertains to

fingering. The score presents us with a picture of how the music should sound, not how it feels in our bodies. The composer does his or her best to convey to us by means of notational symbols which notes to play with which hand. But this is not etched in stone, despite my colleague's insistence that it would be cheating to re-divide the labor. Consider the third measure of Example 9-3 below. Neither of the editor's suggested fingerings is satisfactory for a smooth execution. Try this. Play the lower right hand B flat, which occurs on the second beat, with the left hand thumb and use the fingering I put underneath. Re-dividing is not cheating and sometimes feels much nicer.

Example 9-3 Beethoven Appassionata, 3rd Movmnt. Re-divide Between Hands.

Ready for a few more advanced ideas? Octaves should not be fingered. We can create the illusion of *legato* using pedal and a combination of rotation and grouping. Even in large hands, fingering octaves 3-4-5 or just 4-5 creates unnatural strain, particularly in speed and when repetitive practicing is involved. Finger octaves with all fives. Rapid repeated notes are best articulated by beginning each group with the thumb followed by 3 and 2 (triplets) or followed by 4,3,2 (quadruplets). Note that the hand will need to be at a slight angle with the keyboard and there will be rotation and slight in and out movements. Play chromatic thirds by repeating the thumb and crossing a longer finger over a shorter finger.

TEN

ON RELAXATION AT THE PIANO

A student explains that when he returned to the piano after a long break because of injury, he intentionally chose pieces that were not physically demanding. He felt he had a tendency toward over-use injuries and wanted to take it easy.

Some four years later he is injury free except for some soreness that develops when he wants to "let go." But he feels he has the same tendencies he had to overcome when learning to trill, which is to tighten up. *Relaxing* (my italics) in this circumstance seems even more challenging for him.

One should be able to play any music without over-use issues. One should be able to "let go" musically without experiencing soreness. When the required movements are well understood and well worked-in, they become second nature, requiring almost no conscious thought. This leaves the mind free to express, through this technical skill, what the psyche demands. It should become like breathing, which we do in the background while performing all our other tasks. If the breathing experiences disruption, the body complains to the brain—it's a call to arms. It should be the same with technique.

I think that if this student wants to relax, he should go to a spa and have a massage. He appears to have some misunderstanding about how the playing mechanism works. *Relax* is just as problematic as *tense* when it comes to playing the piano. Relaxation is not a tool for playing the piano. It is more a result; it is what happens in the wake of correct physical action. We can't really direct individual flexors or abductors to relax or flex. Our bodies contain opposing muscles in every limb, so stretching to extremes will force those opposing muscles to act against each other and create unnecessary tension. My teacher used to say that if you think *relax* you'll fall off the piano bench, meaning that the term is too general. Her answer was to find out how much of a given mechanical solution is needed, which is always very little, to produce the desired result.

Try this. For the tiniest second, stretch your hand to an extreme. Stop! Now have someone take your loose hand and open it for you. Notice the difference in the way it feels? Notice, too, that with this outside help you can actually extend a little farther. This is called *passive resistance*. We can let the piano open our hands sometimes and it can be a big help.

When a problem is at first solved, students very often want to exaggerate the motion. This is not necessarily a bad idea at first, as the slight exaggeration can help teach the concept to the muscles involved. But when something feels right, more of it does not make it better. So it is important to direct one's attention to how the fingers, hand and arm are aligned and what kind of movement is required, for example, to transfer the weight of the arm from one finger to the next. This automatically replaces the general thinking (relax/tense) with specific movements that can be monitored and controlled. The end result is a feeling of virtually no feeling at all; it is as if the fingers are moving slowly, though the passage is quick.

This student mentions a tightening up when trying to trill, not an uncommon syndrome. If reduced to its components, a trill is nothing more than a series of notes that change direction with each note. So, the basic underlying technique is rotation. But remember what we learned about a long series of notes? They need a pulse. Trills are usually indicated with a symbol, but no help is given as to how many notes are to be included. Here's something to file away in the hard-drive of your memory: All ornaments indicated by symbols instead of actual notes and rhythms, including appoggiaturas and other groups of small notes, still need a place in time. That is, tell your hand how many notes to play, in what rhythm and where do these rhythms fall against the pulse in the other hand. Sometimes the execution of long trills can be facilitated by using 1-3, in which case the wrist is a little lower than usual and there can be a tiny *in* shape (for the thumb) and *out* again

If this student is serious about wanting to correct these issues, I think some retraining is in order. How much effort does it really take to stand on one note or to walk from that note to the next?

ELEVEN

ON PROJECTING AT THE PIANO

A pianist asks:

1. How would you define this word *projection* and what distinguishes a piano or pianist with good projection?

2. Some say good projection is the piano's (or pianist's) ability to be heard in a large hall even if they're "playing softly". Some say that when a pianist is playing a *pianissimo* passage in a large hall, those who project well are just playing that passage more loudly (if one were standing right next to the piano). Some say good projection is the ability of the pianist or piano to project over an orchestra, which, to me, implies a certain degree of loudness (without becoming very unpleasant) or brightness in the piano. Do you agree with either or both of these concepts of good projection?

3. If you think good projection is mostly due to the piano, can you describe why certain pianos have this quality? If you think it's mostly due to the pianist, what in their playing determines whether a pianist will have good projection?

4. Is the idea of projection only applicable to performances in rather large halls? (I can't see how this concept would apply in the home or in a small hall.)

My response: Projection has to do with both the piano and the pianist. The duller the former is, the sharper the latter has to be. The acoustical properties of the hall can also be a large issue. But projection is also about conveying the ideas of the music to the listener. Imagine standing on a stage and speaking of love to someone in the last row of a hall. You would use your voice differently than if the person were standing next to you. Similarly, in your living room you would speak differently to someone across the room than you would if he were next to you. This is about loudness, but also about focus. Noted pedagogue John Crown used to say that when we play we listen with three ears: one for the sound on stage, one for the concept inside our heads and one at the back of the hall.

Sound carries when the appropriate amount of weight and impetus are applied. This is about loudness, but also about quality.

If we accept the physicist's notion that the number and prominence of overtones determine quality, then we have to consider how to control the overtones. Playing with a *cushioned* attack from the key will produce fewer upper partials in the overtone series than will striking the key hard and fast from above. Remember, the upper partials become closer together the higher in the series you go, becoming quite dissonant at the top. String players are well aware of this physical characteristic of vibrating strings, as they are often called upon to produce harmonics by stopping the string from vibrating at various points along the string's surface. We use both types of attacks—cushioned and percussive—in order to control the *meaning* of the sound, the ideas we want to convey to the listener. The brighter the sound, the one produced by moving more quickly into the key and with more weight, the more likely it will carry. The manner in which we voice our chords, that is, showing the notes that are most prominent, will also have an impact.

Consider the oboe. It famously produces a small, "narrow" sound, but its quality and range can make it very piercing. Whereas the double bass has a thicker, "wider" sound and lower range, perhaps even louder in terms of decibels (not sure about that), and yet it is very difficult to hear clearly in a hall. So, depending on our musical intentions, the nature of the piano and the hall, we have to decide on what kind of attack will produce the desired results.

Practically speaking, in our rehearsing we should always listen with that 3rd ear for what I call a *usable* sound, one that speaks beyond the immediate environment of the instrument, often referred to as a singing sound. This needs to be worked into the technique just like any other skill. Sometimes students play on the surface of the keys; I call this whispering or talking to oneself. Our objective as performers is to create various illusions, one of which is the illusion of whispering, a stage whisper to put it in acting terms, achieved by combining the appropriate amount of weight and speed of key descent. That third ear tells us what is needed for a particular hall; the stage ear tells us what is needed for a particular piano. And the inner ear governs all of the above.

TWELVE

ON SIGHT READING

There is really no such thing as *sight-reading*. Sight-reading consists of learning to recognize already familiar patterns that are put together in different ways, very much like the way letters are put together to form words. This sounds like evasion, I know, but if you consider the topic with this idea in mind, you will conclude that the best way to learn to sight-read well is to do it on a regular basis, the way you learned to read words.

I know this is how I developed my reading skills. From my first piano book, *The Adult at the Piano* by Bernice Frost, which started us out, as I recall, with the grand staff, I was armed with the ability to associate note-heads with keys of the piano and I was off and running through any literature I could get my hands on. The down side of this, my first teachers would probably point out, is that I read through all my books and wanted new ones. This was not conducive to actual practicing. Now that I think about it, not practicing in an organized way may have been a good thing, as I didn't have the opportunity to pick up so many habits that would have to be unlearned later. And incidentally, being a fluent sight-reader will open many doors, sometimes-lucrative ones.

There are sight-reading exercises available that approach the topic in this way, gradually increasing the types of figures that are combined. But I've concluded that this approach is too dry and unmusical. It's best to have available some pieces that are several levels easier than what one can actually play, and spend ten minutes of the practice time reading them.

Some procedures:

- Scan the piece before playing, noticing the composer's directions and any oddities, i.e., accidentals, tempo changes, etc.
- Think of a tempo that should work for the quickest passages.
- Set that tempo and don't stop for anything. If you have trouble, go to the next beat or next measure, but keep the pulse going. Teacher-student duets are great for this and

there are many such collections: Diabelli Op. 149 & Op. 163; *Four Centuries of Piano Duet Music* by Cameron McGraw in four volumes and graded for difficulty. These are not transcriptions, but rather original pieces for piano duet.

- Make a conscious decision from the start to try to notice all musical directions in the score: dynamics, articulation, etc.
- Keep eyes on the music, not on the hands.
- Always look ahead in the score, not at what has just been played.
- Make no mental judgments while playing. Do a *post mortem* afterwards, if you must.
- Keep in mind that the objective is to make music, not just rattle off notes.

THIRTEEN

MUSICIANS ARE SMARTER

In case you were wondering whether to practice today or not, please read on: A new study found that musicians might have brains that function better than their peers well into old age.

This is summarized from a Huffington Post article, which can be read in full at HuffingtonPost.com under the title *Musicians Are Probably Smarter Than the Rest of Us.*

Researchers tested the mental abilities of senior citizens and discovered that musicians performed better at a number of tests. In particular, musicians excelled at visual memory tasks. While musicians had similar verbal capabilities to non-musicians, the musicians' ability to memorize new words was markedly better, too. Perhaps most importantly, the musicians' IQ scores were higher overall than those who spent their lives listening to music rather than performing it.

The experience of musicians also played a role in how sharp their minds were. The younger the musicians were when they began to play their instruments, the better their minds performed at the mental tasks. Additionally, the total number of years musicians played instruments throughout their life corresponded with how strong their brains remained years later.

The study also found that musicians who took the time to exercise between symphonies had even higher-functioning brain capabilities. This finding supports another recent study that reported people who walk regularly maintain healthier brains. With that in mind, perhaps joining a marching band now will make you the smartest person at the retirement home in the future.

A summary of the original research goes something like this: While it is known that practicing music repeatedly changes the organization of the brain, it is not clear if these changes can correlate musical abilities with non-musical abilities. The study of 70 older participants, with different musical experience over their lifetimes, provides a connection between musical activity and mental balance in old age. "The results of this preliminary study revealed that participants with at least 10 years of musical experience (high activity musicians) had better performance in nonverbal memory, naming, and executive processes in advanced age relative to non-musicians."

No, I won't discuss my age in print. Suffice it to say, though, that I've lived long enough to suspect that these findings are accurate, and my brain is working just fine, thank you—despite any indications to the contrary that you may have found in this book.

FOURTEEN

ON LIFTING THE FINGERS

A student writes:

I've started some new finger strengthening/independence exercises and my left pinky is giving me some trouble. In one exercise, I have all five fingers of left hand pressed down onto keyboard bed (proper wrist position, etc) and I hold 4 fingers down while taking the 5th finger and playing the key a certain number of times (16-20) with one finger- up and down, etc.

It's no wonder her pinky is giving her trouble. She has a misunderstanding about how the fingers work. They don't want to play by lifting away from the hand; they want to play by rotating into the key with the forearm behind them. The 5th and 4th fingers are much maligned when called weak. There is nothing wrong with them. We pianists don't train for strength the way athletes do; we train for coordination of refined muscles. It takes very little physical strength to play the piano. She is definitely on the wrong track when holding down other fingers and lifting her 5th away from the hand. (Dohnany wrote some exercises along this line, which I think are destructive.)

The fingers gain strength by having the forearm behind them. This is achieved with the 5th by slightly rotating the forearm toward it. The motion is rotary, like turning a doorknob. See Chapter One.

The inference behind her misunderstanding is a familiar one. It's those old wives again. They repeat over and over again what they think they see happening. They see fingers moving and with little or no understanding they make assumptions about what is causing the movement. They hear clear articulation and they think, "Aha, independent fingers." The fingers are not physically independent of one another, but they can be made to sound that way by aligning them properly with the hand and arm. *Finger independence!* Let's banish this term from the vocabulary. How about *fingers sounding independent* instead?

I hope she doesn't hurt herself.

FIFTEEN

ON COMPETITIONS

MAKING MUSIC IS NOT A COMPETITIVE SPORT

At J. conservatory, the students of Mme. L. always won the concerto competition. It was expected; it was the norm. The student contestants expected it. Mme expected it. The entire school expected it. Yet, all of the teachers entered their students, pressing them into this futile exercise. Student X., a friend of mine who studied with Mr. F., prepared the concerto *du jour*, Mozart Coronation, to the exclusion of virtually his entire repertoire. He was an obsessive/compulsive personality, as it seems many of the students were in those days (probably still are) and prepared as if his life depended on it. He told me he didn't want to disappoint Mr. F, but I know from other conversations that his unsupportive parents figured in the mix. His mother once visited his room near the school and pronounced it the product of a sick mind. Well, student X. told me, maybe this time a different teacher would produce the winning performer. Wouldn't that be an upheaval? Maybe Mr. F. would get the respect he deserves.

The piano faculty assembled, along with Maestro M. and his conducting staff. The students congregated in the corridors, where they waited for their time to audition. Some, of course, would be in the practice rooms up to the last possible minute; student X. was one of these. As a graduate student, I was somewhat above the fray. I'd lived enough to know that life didn't depend on only one performance, or on any one event, unless that event included being run over by a bus.

Student X. appeared on the scene just seconds before his appointed time. I was there to listen from outside, as he had asked, and gave him by best thumbs-up smile. He played like an angel. They let him play the entire concerto through, including the cadenzas, which I took to be a good sign. I waited by the stage entrance to congratulate him but when the door opened, X. ran right past me muttering "I missed a note, I missed a note" over and over all the way to the men's room, where he vomited violently. Student X. played like an artist, suffered terribly and the winning contestant did not come from the studio of Mr. F. that year.

Student X. was last seen on a Kibbutz in Israel. In this case, the jury lived up to its pretrial publicity.

Some would argue that this sort of pressure simulates life, that it prepares students for what they will face in the real world. It's true that only those who are strong enough in personality—those who really need to perform in public—will succeed in big careers as concert performers. This has been my experience. But what a pity that some very fine talents fall by the wayside in this competitive process.

As an adjudicator, I've been in the difficult position of having to declare one pianist a winner over all the others, when several deserve recognition. It seems a given that when one wins, the others lose, or are thought of as losers, when this is far from the case. Once I was on a panel that heard five young pianists in a row play very compelling *Fantasie Impromptus*, Chopin, all technically precise and each with an individual take on the piece. Someone had to win, though. On another occasion we heard college-age contestants play several Prokofief thirds in a row (I excised that concerto from my life afterwards), all of which deserved to win. Yet, again, we had to declare some to be losers.

Let's focus on music, not try to single out who is better than whom. I know, I know. Our world is such that we feel compelled to create stars, to experience the excitement of the race and declare a winner. Winning can be how careers are made, but this happens rather more rarely than one might think. And of course, auditions are the way to hear what a person can do. Let's not pit one against another, though, but rather declare all who've achieved excellence to be winners, deserving of an audience. Let's create a musical democracy, where winners can come from any corner, from any teacher's studio. If you give life to the music, you've won.

Which brings me to a final point about playing the piano. Does music only live in public performance? This question is akin to the problem of a tree falling in the forest. When the piano is played live, though, there is always an audience, only the size varies, from thousands to just the player. I maintain that the ability to play the piano, even at virtuoso levels, can be quite separate from being able to perform in public at the same level. I know of many fine pianists who are not fine performers. That is, for them performing in public is a struggle, a struggle with nerves, self-doubt, lack of support in their private lives or as children. You name it. This of course diminishes the pleasure they experience playing in public, and indeed, discourages them from doing so. It's a pity of course not to be able to easily share one's accomplishments with the general public. But the satisfaction to be had at playing in informal house concerts or even for one's students or one's self, should not be underestimated, and it is still worth the trouble to perfect the art and having done so, pass it on.

SIXTEEN

PRODUCING SYNCHRONIZED CHORDS

A student wrote to me complaining of *wobbly* chords. He meant that in accompaniment passages of repeated chordal figures he often broke the chords unintentionally. Apparently, some fingers reached the point of sound before others. His solution was to rigidify his fingers, lifting the unneeded fingers away from his hand, in order to force the correct fingers to play simultaneously. This is no solution at all, but rather a prescription for disaster.

In order to accommodate different finger lengths, it is better to allow the hand to be slightly flatter and avoid gripping or locking the hand into a fixed position in order to force all the fingers to be the same lengths. No matter how hard you try, I promise you that the fingers will always be different lengths. By *flatter* I mean that the hand should maintain its normal curvature, not curled into a claw.

The manner of depressing the key, then, is downward, of course, but also *slightly* in the direction of out toward the torso. It is as if the intention is to move outward, but at the point of key contact there is a tread on the end of the fingers playing that prevents an extreme slide outward. It is not necessary to leave the surface of the key. In fact, it is in most cases better after depressing the key to ride it back up just beyond the point of sound in order to repeat it. This has the effect of allowing the participation of the forearm, ever so slightly, in order to control the downward weight. It is a mistake to think of this as either just a finger movement or a wrist movement. If the accompaniment pattern is a repetition of the same chord, make a slight in and out shape. That is, find a slightly different spot on the keys as you allow them to rise up just past the point of sound.

Try this in various combinations of white and black keys, listening for voicing, in which the feeling is one of depressing the prominent pitch deeper than the other pitches. I visualize making slight indentations with my fingertips in damp sand, where one of the fingers goes a bit deeper than the others. What is actually happening at the piano, though, is a redistribution of weight.

As we have already learned, in no case should some fingers be lifted away from the hand while others are held down. Rather think of the arm and hand as a single unit, with the weight distributed as needed to the fingers required.

There was a time in the 19th century when rolled chords were considered expressive, even if not indicated by the composer. It is, I think, still a default expressive devise used unconsciously by pianists straining to show how musical they are. This I put into a category of wasted effort, along with people who disappear in order to show how musical they are.

The problem as described by this student, though, sounds like a legitimate technical issue that needs attention.

SEVENTEEN

THE PRESSURE OF THE PRACTICE ROOM PEER

IT'S REALLY NOT A COMPETITION

A student traveling abroad wrote to me of his experience at Steinway, where he had rented a practice room. My student is fairly new to formal piano study, though he has worked on his own for many months. He has the advantage of being able to learn repertoire very quickly and is able to play quite creditably several of the WTC, all movements of the Moonlight Sonata and a few of the Chopin Nocturnes, all from a very secure memory. (I find this ability to be remarkable.)

He found himself in a room next to a much more experienced pianist who was practicing a modern, very complicated-sounding piece, which had an intimidating effect on my student. He apparently began to feel inadequate, even to the point of not being able to remember the pieces he had come to practice.

So let me say this: Comparisons with other pianists are both inevitable and futile. It can turn you into a ghost. Try to avoid listening to other pianists playing your repertoire (I know!). If you do listen to recordings, listen to more than one performance of the same piece in order to prove to yourself there can be differences in approaches. This will give you permission to be your own pianist. Go to live performances when possible, as these are more human and can be very instructive. When I was working on the Liszt sonata, I had the opportunity to hear Emil Gilels play it in Los Angeles. It was a piece he had recorded and was known for. Well, it was a wonderful performance in many ways, but not at all pristine. Over the years, I've had many such experiences hearing the great and famous appear in public as human beings. Finally, try to limit your comparisons to yourself of today with yourself of before. Revel in your progress and this will give you courage. We have to evaluate our performances in order to make progress, so take note of your needs (notice I don't say weaknesses). Be kind to yourself in the process.

My student says he left early because he just couldn't

concentrate; this practice peer had ruined the whole thing. And when he snuck a peek into the neighboring room he saw a young Asian man, dancing wildly at the keyboard, and looking everywhere *but* the keys. "Seriously I don't know how his fingers found the notes, he was moving so much." My student had the impression that this other pianist could play any repertoire with ease and his own efforts, my student's, seemed to pale in comparison.

The pressure of practice-room peers! This is something most music students in conservatories have to deal with. But since my student hadn't been in a formal music school, he had no experience of this. It takes getting used to. I remember the practice room days when there would be a constant awareness that someone could hear what I was doing. Sometimes, it was difficult to resist the urge to perform, instead of practice, which are of course two different activities.

What really is at issue is the ability to focus and concentrate on what you have before you. It takes a fair amount of discipline sometimes not to be drawn into someone else's work. But this is, after all, what we have to learn to do for successful public performance. And it is not a reasonable assumption that this other pianist would be able to do your work better or even as well as you. But even that is of no consequence. Your practicing is only about you. Patience with the self is a necessity for improvement. I advised my student to try it again.

Side note: It's not necessary to look at the keys at all in order to play with accuracy. We have among us exemplary pianists who are without sight.

EIGHTEEN

ON THE VALUE OF EXERCISES

A pianist writes in a forum: "I have been told by some pianists that Hanon's *The Virtuoso Pianist, In Sixty Exercises* is a waste of time.... it's stupid and nonsense. One pianist even asked me, 'Do you think Tchaikovsky or Mozart played these? Throw the book away.' On the other hand, a piano student studying for her doctorate in piano performance told me that she plays them every day and that she believes it helps her playing. What is the general consensus on this? I believe if it works for you then by all means play it. However if that's the case then should all teachers teach all their students Hanon?"

My response: What do you mean by *works for you*? When playing something (an exercise) that is supposed to prepare you for something else (a piece of music), I think it's important to ask yourself why? What is the purpose of this particular exercise?

Unfortunately, Mr. Hanon only gives metronome indications and says to repeat the exercises. He doesn't really tell us how to play the exercises, except to lift the fingers high (!). He tells us that they will produce agility, strength (!), independence and evenness. They won't do any of that by lifting fingers high and if you are overly diligent, these activities can cause you harm.

The mindset from which this point of view stems has largely been discredited over the years, although some still cling doggedly to it, i.e., that it takes physical strength to play the piano. It does not. A small child can do it. And here again is a central theme of this book; we gain power not by lifting the fingers away from the hand, which is something they weren't designed to do efficiently, but rather by dropping into the keys with the discreet participation of the forearm. Hanon's supposition is that by lifting the fingers they will become strong and independent, but we don't train the way weight lifters train, by building muscle mass. Rather, we train for refined coordination. The fingers never will be independent of each other, nor need they be; they can, however, be made to sound that way.

In short, "you can play whatever you want, dear," to quote my teacher, but once you know how to play the exercises correctly, i.e., with the participation of the forearm, there is no longer any reason to play them. In fact, there's no point in playing them at all because the technical issues can be addressed in music.

As for the doctoral candidate, that routine may serve several purposes: Provide a comforting and mindless routine, a delay tactic for avoiding the requisite thinking or some other obsessive/compulsive purpose. In graduate school I knew a wonderful pianist who drilled scales for hours. Her scales were indeed perfection and she played the 4th Beethoven concerto like a master. But the same compulsion that drove her to drill those scales, and they were beautiful, drove her into some sort of breakdown and when I last heard she had given up the piano entirely and joined a protective order of some sort. Admittedly, that is an extreme case and this particular pianist was apparently troubled. Playing Hanon won't necessarily cause so severe a reaction and probably won't case any particular harm, unless the idea of lifting fingers is taken to extremes.

Later in the post someone writes:
> "Any system, method, or approach is only as good as the teacher and the student practicing. The success probably goes beyond the method. I think that if something is repetitive, and if the person practicing it is wrongly guided or self-guides, there might be harm because a wrong motion done repeatedly will hurt. At the same time, if a right motion is well-guided, then you have a well-practiced set of right motions that will serve you well."

My Response: You are right. But just as the success goes beyond the method, so too do the failures. By failures I mean conceptual misunderstandings. Perhaps this is what you mean by practicing "wrongly." But it's more than practicing wrongly. Please don't think I'm just being argumentative here. I'm genuinely concerned about this issue.

The concept inherent in exercises in general is that repetition of note patterns will create strong fingers or independent fingers or that these patterns will occur in the same way in music. These ideas date from the 1880's and have their origins in the experience of keyboard players who were steeped in harpsichord techniques. I believe Czerny and Hanon and the others were probably sincere, although I don't completely discount the notion that money was to be made off of the burgeoning piano market. When Hanon, for example, was popular and adopted by so many institutions, Matthay had not yet written about the use of the forearm. Keyboard players thought primarily about lifting fingers, despite Schumann's unfortunate experience. (Google Landowska's photo of her claw-like hands. She was a remarkable artist, but those hands speak volumes.)

If you discard Hanon's "instructions," as I believe all pianists should, the exercises can be used to show how patterns can be grouped together for technical ease, how to shape. But you can learn these techniques in a Mozart sonata. If you don't believe in lifting the fingers away from the hand (as he instructs) or training for strength and therefore using repetition for endurance (wrong concepts), then I implore you to ask yourself what specifically do you hope to gain by practicing Hanon.

Let me be clear: I don't think the exercises themselves are dangerous, unless done to an extreme, or carcinogenic, as some have suggested, but the underlying concepts that students take away are not in sync with a system of playing that uses the body efficiently, the way it was designed to be used. Students invariably take away the idea that repetition of patterns is the key to success, when the *working-in* of specific, local and correct physical movements is the key to success. By *local* I mean what do the finger, hand, arm—working as a unit— do in this spot to get easily and efficiently from here to there? This, of course, requires knowledge of the working mechanism, but, as we have seen, one doesn't have to be a doctor.

It is possible to play the piano with great success using many different points of view, or from no point of view at all. I choose to use a specific physical approach that allows my hands to be used according to their design. The fingers are strong and sound independent if the forearm is allowed to play its part, and there is nothing wrong with the 4th finger, just in case anyone was wondering.

At some point in the development of a young pianist it becomes necessary to consider how to advance technically. I propose selecting music appropriate to the level and technical needs of the student. Sadly, this requires more thought and preparation from the teacher, inspiration even. But we are lucky to have today, 150 years after Hanon, many fine publications of very serviceable music available for the choosing. Imagine.

NINETEEN

TO CZERNY OR NOT TO CZERNY

ON CZERNY VS CHOPIN

A student asks which Czerny studies he should select in preparation for Chopin *Etudes*. This student has already played all movements of the Moonlight sonata.

My Response: The Chopin *Etudes* are concert pieces, and in that regard somewhat misnamed. Chopin, I'm quite sure, wasn't thinking pedagogically, about building a technique. Having said that, however, one can learn a great deal studying them, just as we learn technique studying any piece.

I think Czerny and studies of that ilk are largely a waste of time (see Chapter Eighteen). They have in their genesis the notion that repetition builds strength and endurance, a notion long since discredited by pianists who've given it any thought. We don't build strength in larger muscles so much as we train muscles for refined coordination. So, I'd rather he use his time working out technique in the Chopin, even if he doesn't get them up to top tempo first time around. The Revolutionary, Op. 10, No. 12, is a good place to start. I also like F major from Op. 10 for the right hand.

For an *etude* on the two-note slur, have a look at the Tempest sonata of Beethoven, first movement.

Here I'd like to make a proposal. An excellent idea for a doctoral dissertation in pedagogy would be to supplant Czerny and Hanon with collections of *etudes* culled from excerpts in the standard piano repertoire. That way, we could do away entirely with the notion that it is necessary to practice X in order to achieve Y. Each selection should provide training in particular concepts along the lines discussed here and could be progressive in difficulty. By the end of the study, the student would have music to play and not just some unpresentable closet exercises.

TWENTY

FULL STICK, SHORT STICK, OR NO STICK

THE PIANO IN CHAMBER ENSEMBLE

An unhappy amateur string player writes: "So many pianists love to play with strings, but have little awareness of appropriate voicing. Young professional groups have the same problem, using a full stick that overpowers the sound."

I feel (hear) his pain. There is nothing worse than playing one's heart out only to have it trod upon by inconsiderate colleagues. Every player wants his/her lovely inflections to be heard and responded to musically. I think the operative word here is consideration, which is about listening to one another and not about the length of the piano stick. I write as a professional collaborative pianist and amateur string player.

The piano sounds muted if the lid is closed. This would be similar to the string players putting on their mutes, and no one wants to play like that. The short stick can be a solution if the piano is particularly bright and the room is small. But the raised lid is not so much about volume as it is about quality of sound. And here is where the importance of listening comes into play. Very often in amateur groups, the pianist can feel so overwhelmed with the difficulties of his part that there is a disconnect between the ear and the hands. The obvious solution here is that the pianist learns his part.

But let's say the pianist is in control of the notes and is free to listen. He should be able to hear his colleagues, especially the leading voice(s), just slightly above what he is playing, keeping in mind that the music rack blocks much of what he hears of himself. If he hears his colleagues free and clear, well above what he is playing, then he is too soft and not playing as a full partner. And, of course, if he doesn't hear them at all, he is too loud.

The string player points out: "Chamber Music has traditionally been played on small instruments in intimate settings. After all, pianos originated in the quiet voices of seventeenth and eighteenth century harpsichords and clavichords."

Any pianist can obliterate any string player sonically. This is a given. It is, however, misleading to equate modern instruments with those of the 18th century. Early keyboard instruments were indeed more demure, but so were their string colleagues. Whether the development of these instruments into their modern counterparts was proportional I can't really say, although I suspect the piano made greater strides with its concert hall sizes and the introduction of metal harps. I have to say, though, that's it's a rare situation to find a concert grand housed in a private setting. So size isn't very often an issue.

Let's make a very general assessment of the repertoire. In the classical period strings began as an obbligato addition to the piano part, sometimes only doubling the piano. This is particularly prevalent in many Haydn trios and all but a hand full of Mozart violin sonatas. In the Mozart piano quartets, the piano part is very concerto like. With Beethoven, even already in Op. 1, we begin to get a more equal division of labor. And in the 19th century, finally, we get sonorities of strings vs. piano in passionate struggle. (I'm thinking of Brahms.) Chamber music has traditionally been played in parlors, in intimate settings, yet the music itself has evolved into anything but intimate.

Finally, a word about the practical nature of the setup. The cellists, of whom I am one, complain the loudest. We are usually placed right in the bend of the piano, where we are pummeled with sound. What we hear next to us, though, is probably not what a listener several feet away hears. It's natural for musicians to play to the room and not to the person sitting next to him. Because of all that glorious sound in his ear, the cellist feels the need to either play forcefully all the time or make threatening grimaces at the poor pianist, when it may not really be his fault. So I always suggest if feasible, that the strings find positions somewhat away from the piano. Or, alternatively, rethink the nature of projection and play for each other instead of for the room.

In concert halls I have heard all periods of music played superbly with appropriate balance, yes, using a concert grand with the stick on full extension.

TWENTY-ONE

ON LEARNING MUSIC QUICKLY

A student of accompanying asks for suggestions on learning repertoire quickly.

Accompanying, a specialty usually referred to these days as the collaborative arts, often demands of its practitioners the ability to learn music under pressure. Unlike the specialist in solo repertoire, the collaborative pianist plays everyone's repertoire, not just a collection of his/her own solos and concertos he has prepared well in advance for a particular concert season. The collaborator must be able to play art songs in many languages—if you're wondering why language matters, remember that the first step in figuring out an accompaniment is to understand the poem—and identical works in several keys in order to accommodate different voice types, often at short or even no advance notice. Add to this already considerable repertoire occasional pieces and instrumental sonatas, often very technically demanding, and the pianist might well find himself locked in the practice room buried under a mountain of scores, never to be seen again.

One important attribute of the successful professional collaborator is the ability to read well at first sight. So, that's where I'll start. In order to improve sight-reading, do it on a daily basis. Elsewhere I discuss reading techniques in some detail, but the basics are these: Scan the piece looking for surprises, set a pulse that will accommodate the fastest passages, always look ahead in the score and not at your hands, keep going no matter what. I recommend keeping some scores handy that are technically somewhat easier than you can really play and use these for 10 minutes of reading in every practice session. And/or, set aside a session for just reading.

Collaborative pianists often live in pigeonholes; they are either vocal accompanists or instrumental accompanists. There's no good reason for this. Instrumental sonatas tend to be technically more challenging, but the vocal accompanist is called upon, more often than not, to be orchestra, conductor, scenic designer and vocal coach. I submit to you, gentle reader, that all of these skills are required for any pianist who hopes to be considered an artist.

This is why I always recommend to my soloist students that they work with other musicians in order to learn to listen not only to themselves, but also to the inner workings of the music they play.

So, soprano Madame La Bella Voce or violinist Tossi Spiccato has called upon you to play this weekend at a gala event and could you please rehearse tomorrow afternoon at their home. They invariably have an ancient piano, of which they are unreasonably proud. The pedals don't work, "But you don't really need them, do you?" (I'm not kidding.) Side note: Invite them to your own studio at a time that suits you. Be sure to inquire about the piano you will play at the event. Will it be tuned? Do they actually have a piano? (Again, I'm not kidding.) Your heart has stopped pounding enough to consider how to begin cramming the repertoire. Do not—I repeat—do not start playing the pieces through over and over again in a blind panic.

Do this: 1. Look through the repertoire list—with any luck at all you will have played some of it already—and select the most technically challenging movement. In this challenging movement, scan through to the end of the piece away from the piano. Note the gnarly places and begin there, as *slowly as you need to and not faster than you can.* Gradually work in this one passage until it is up to a respectable tempo. Then move on to the next place in this same piece or in a different piece until you have covered all of the technical issues. This will give you confidence.

Remember, the first encounter is only a rehearsal. You will need to make an impression on your partner, especially if you are meeting for the first time, and you will need to keep up with him in repertoire that he already knows (presumably). But this first meeting is, ideally, an opportunity to work out issues. You can ask to work on sections that bother you, not just be at the beck and call of your partner. Singers very often need to be led, as in arias, and they need help managing breathing, so work this into your own practicing. The placement of the pianist's beat with singers is on the vowel, a little more sluggish, perhaps, than with a string player who is more likely to be precisely on the beat or a little ahead. This is why we listen. (See the article on raised piano lids for thoughts on balance.)

Do this: 2. Practice focusing on the solo line. If you can play all of your part and sing the solo line, this is great. If not, play just your bass line and sing or play the solo line. This is the single most important skill of the collaborator, I think. That is, to be able to arrive with the partner, adjusting imperceptibly as necessary, on his beat. A well-meaning woman once came to me after a concert and gushed that I was such a fine accompanist, I *followed* so well. It was a nice compliment, of course, but I hasten to point out here that a good accompanist doesn't follow, he *anticipates*. In order to anticipate, the pianist must be inside the solo line at all times.

I am of the opinion that all collaborations are partnerships. However, in the case of instrumental sonatas, both players are equal partners and must give way or lead depending on who has the leading voice. I once played a *duo* recital with a violinist from the Heifetz class, a duo recital because I had been asked to play a Beethoven solo sonata in addition to her repertoire. Her father came to me afterwards and pointed out that the pianist shouldn't share the fee equally, but rather only gets a portion of it. When I explained that I had actually played more than she had, he begrudgingly agreed and we split the fee. No one offered to pay me more, though, for my extra effort. Sigh. (See Gerald Moore, *The Unashamed Accompanist*, for more on fees and other delicious topics.)

Do this: 3. Look for the essence of the piano part. What does it contribute to the overall meaning? This is particularly important in art song, where the piano sets the scene or creates a mood. Consider Schubert's bubbling brooks, horses on the hoof or wind in the wimple. Look for preludes, interludes and postludes, where the piano is featured and make sure that these sections are soloistic and secure. Look also for scene changes and notice where the change occurs. Does the pianist make the change, perhaps during an interlude? Or does the partner do it first? In a well-written piece these changes are clearly audible in the music, but when in doubt, consult the text (with which you are already intimately familiar).

Orchestra reductions, such as arias or concertos, should be made to sound orchestral. I know. We only have a piano. But a piano staccato is sharper and drier than an orchestral staccato. Woodwinds have a different voice, a sharper more defined attack, perhaps, than strings, which can be more cushioned. Above all, though, remember that a reduction is just that; it is someone's idea of how to realize the orchestra at the piano. Your own thoughts about sonority might be just as good or better than the one printed. So don't be afraid to make changes. And certainly don't be constrained by arbitrary technical issues. In arias, where the pianist is orchestra and conductor, he might lead the entire effort, providing the singer with a secure rhythmic foundation. Likewise, in some concerto passages and motoric music, the pianist must just keep a steady beat, without trying to adjust to *rubato* in the solo part. This is particularly true after the first movement cadenza in Mendelssohn's concerto where the violin plays spiccato arpeggios.

Do this: 4. Look for oceans of similarity. Does the piano create waves of sound on E flat for measures on end? Look at it and move on. Ostinato passages can be a lifesaver. Once noticed, they only need repetition. Mark off sections and practice in sections.

Do this: 5. Look for possible ensemble difficulties and make sure you understand the rhythmic connection of the piano part to the other part.

In short, take care to be familiar with *both* parts, how they work together rhythmically and how they play off one another musically. A well-prepared partner will know the piano part in addition to his own.

Learning music in a hurry is not ideal but sometimes is necessary, especially when one's livelihood depends on it. Don't turn down a job because you would rather study the music and rehearse for weeks and know the music inside and out. With determination and thoughtful selective practicing, a fine performance can result and with more experience, even an exemplary performance is possible.

Tip: Learn a song per day from anthologies of Schubert, Schumann, Brahms, Strauss, Fauré and Duparc and you will eventually have a respectable repertoire of often-programmed music. Add Falla and Poulenc as needed. Leave big instrumental sonatas for ad hoc occasions, though Schubert *sonatinas* and Mozart violin and piano sonatas make excellent sight-reading material. Do familiarize yourself with the three Brahms violin sonatas (look at technical spots), the Beethoven Spring and possibly Prokofiev D major.

TWENTY-TWO

WHAT'S IN A SCORE?

NOTATION UNBOUND

No one in his or her right mind condones slavery. I have to ask why, then, do so many accomplished pianists indenture themselves to the printed score? Here are some possible answers. We learn as young piano students to press down a whole note for four counts. We learn that the one, four and five chords can be played broken, as arpeggios. We learn that to play *legato* we have to connect with our fingers. We learn that a short note is *hot* and we have to get off of it. We learn that to travel some distance we have to jump. We learn that every little finger lives in its own little house. Of course, at the time we learn these concepts, they are true, or at least sort of true. These are ways of teaching some of the rudiments of music.

When a pianist becomes an adult, he should put away childish things. It becomes necessary, in the course of adult human events, to hold these truths to be self-evident, that a whole note *sounds* for four counts, but doesn't need to be *held* down when the pedal can do that for us. The one, four and five chords—any chords—when arpeggiated don't require the hand to be blocked, or locked in position because the execution is actually the playing of single notes in succession, not a chord. A finger *legato* is not always achieved by over-holding notes, but can be assisted with subtle use of the pedal. A short note may be created without the idea that the key is burning the finger and must be vacated, but it can be the result of a slight springing action, using the thrust of the key to get to the next note. Great distances are traveled not by thinking of jumping flat-footed, but rather, by springing as from a diving board, using specific mechanisms for achieving lateral movement. The fingers don't occupy their own houses, but rather are fairly itinerant, especially the thumb, which doesn't really live anywhere as a permanent resident. And please don't make your hand into a tennis ball.

So as advanced pianists we learn how to unlearn the lessons of childhood. This brings me to one of my favorite topics; some call it my cipher. The score is our musical bible. From it comes nearly everything we need for a performance, everything except our understanding of historical context. We rely on it to convey to us the composer's expressive intentions, and we should consider carefully every marking as we travel through time, opening our consciousness to the voice of the composer. It is not, however, the composer's intention to tell us how the music should feel in our bodies. The score is a picture of the music. It is not a straight jacket.

Look again at Example 9-3. If we bind ourselves to the notation, the passage can be quite uncomfortable. Re-dividing the labor between the hands as indicated can make it much more fluid. In Example 4-3, are we really going to hold down the half notes in the left hand, even with the pedal marking from the composer? If in Example 4-1 you prefer a *legato* connection from G to C instead of articulating the leap, even here, yes, in Bach, the pedal can discretely touch the G and release again when the C is depressed. The left hand won't register a blur. However, I prefer the articulation between the two notes.

Here's my favorite example of good intentions gone wrong. Notice in Example 22-1 that the homophonic writing, marked *legato* with the instruction to play tenderly, gives rise to the instinct to cling to each chord, the way an organist might. The simple truth is that hinging at the outside fingers in each hand and releasing the other notes of the chords can achieve the desired effect beautifully and effortlessly. Rotate then to each succeeding chord. In other words, let go of everything except the soprano and the bass and assist the *legato* by using a syncopated pedal. This

Example 22-1 Brahms Sonata Violin and Piano A Major.

also makes it easier to sing the melody and show the bass line. Do this right, and I promise the violinist will be hard-pressed to match your mood. You'll make the day.

In Chapter Nine we saw that re-dividing between the hands as an aspect of fingering can facilitate the execution of a complex passage. Here is an example of a passage that, if one is note bound, will be difficult, even impossible to play. It gives me a headache

Example 22-2 Chopin Ballade F Minor. Note Bound.

just looking at it and I've actually worked it out and performed it. First, the rhythm. Play triplets in both hands. The dotted rhythm notation in the left hand was for Chopin, as well as Schubert and others, a shortcut for writing triplets. Now for the nitty-gritty. Ignore the printed fingering and do this: In the right hand, start with thumb on A, then 2-4 on the chord, fifth finger on A. That's right only the one chord in the right hand. In the left hand, start with the fifth finger on E-flat, and then play G-flat and D together as a chord. Move through the ascending octaves in a similar fashion, starting on thumb in the right hand and five in the left hand. Can you apply other concepts here? What about grouping? Shaping? Will the thumb move from a black key to a white key? What about five in the left hand? Does it alternate between black and white? Be sure to lean in the direction of the music in order to avoid moving into a twist. Endnotes:

- The score shows us how the music sounds, not how it feels in our bodies.
- Re-divide between the hands to facilitate execution.
- Let go of long notes as needed, especially if the pedal is also employed.
- Avoid clinging to chords in homophonic passages.

TWENTY-THREE

ON PLAYING OCTAVES

THEY SAID IT COULDN'T BE DONE

Inevitably, when I speak to groups of piano teachers, someone will ask about how to play octaves. This is a topic that is easy for me to overlook because it is really just about playing staccato. The same techniques for springing from one note to the next apply in octave playing. Did I hear a gasp? Yes, it's true, even *legato* octaves.

But first a digression. Early in my tenure at the University of Texas at El Paso we had the very distinct honor of hosting the distinguished pianist John Browning on our campus for a public master class. He came to town to play with the symphony, Mozart Jeunehomme concerto and Ravel concerto for the left hand. He played splendidly. At the class, someone asked him how he managed quick octave passages, which he explained as a wrist action while I sank down in my seat. Then, he sat down to demonstrate and though his wrist showed flexibility, I could see because of my training, that *wrist action* was in fact not the best way to describe what he did.

A number of thoughts come immediately to mind. Great pianists often don't really know how they do what they do. Horowitz famously remarked when asked to join the faculty of the Juilliard School that he didn't know how he did it and so wouldn't know what to say to the students. He showed a remarkable awareness, not to mention honesty. Often these great pianists come from a prodigious background, one in which everything comes easily and naturally from early childhood. I've often thought that this is the best evidence of reincarnation. I had one such prodigy child in my studio some years ago and it was a sobering experience.

Now consider this. Because they are great pianists, students seek them out for advice. Do you see where I'm going with this? If these great pianists were prodigies, chances are they don't have much to offer in the way of technical advice. But by all means, listen to their thoughts on musical style and how to develop a career. Play for them to get their opinions on interpretation or what they think you should tackle next. Put their names in your résumé. But listen with a grain of salt to their comments on execution. This is not to say that there is nothing of value in these comments, just that one may have to filter them through your own understanding of what the body can do.

Browning's comment that octaves come from wrist action is understandable, in a way, because that's sort of what it looks like in speed. But I'll say this at the outset: Don't *initiate* octaves from the wrist. The keys are depressed by the finger/hand/arm alliance. Everything else is more or less supportive. Spring from one octave to the next by means of the staccato action we learned about in the chapter on leaps. Use the diving board to propel you to the next octave, whether it is a neighbor or a distant cousin. Feel a slight hinge in the fifth finger and rotate into the new octave. When moving from white key to white key, travel laterally. When moving from to white to black, think of the diagonal from *out* to *in* and vice versa when moving from black to white. To play octaves in speed, reduce the feeling of individual octaves by grouping them and by giving the groups an overall shape. When possible, play alternating white to black octaves along the black/white border. This reduces most of the in and out motion.

Here's a brief side note. It's hard to argue in the face of a distinguished pianist like John Browning and artists who choose to guess at what it is they do. But it's always interesting and sometimes even worthwhile to read accounts of their training written by concert pianists. A noted pianist has a thoughtful personal history article in the April 8, 2013, issue of *New Yorker* magazine. He caught my attention with: "Learning to play the piano is learning to reason with your muscles." Well okay, I thought. Not a bad way to put it. But then, discussing smooth thumb crossings, he spoiled it with: "[My teacher] devised a symmetrical, synchronous, soul-destroying exercise for this, in which the right and left thumbs reached under the other fingers, crablike, for ever more distant notes." I know this exercise, if it's the same one I came across years ago. Well, fine, surely a pianist as skilled as this one will have some hesitancy here. But then he goes on: "Exercises like this are crucial and yet seem intended to quell any natural enthusiasm for music, or possibly even for life."

Well, maybe this exercise and its penchant for quelling enthusiasms deterred this fully emerged concert artist from spending much time with it. To see him play, you wouldn't think he ever gave any thought to straining his hands. They are beautiful to behold and seem to move efficiently and effortlessly in the service of music.

Here may be the appropriate place to reference what I call *musical masochism*. He continues: "That was the summer music died [a period of time with a teacher]—long, tedious lessons solely on scales, arpeggios, repeated notes, chords. But this misery proved a success.... I'm the sort of person who, if he has to suffer, wants to suffer full time." It's possible that this pianist credits his period of suffering with the success he enjoys today. And who can say with certainty that what he learned in the process hasn't stood him in good stead in some way. He seems to have escaped physical injury, though I suspect the damage to his psyche may be considerable. Here's the pity: It's very likely that he passes on these technical suggestions to his students, in which case the old wives win.

Some personalities accept the notion—victims of another wives' tale, perhaps—that artists must suffer for their art. Suffer emotionally, if you want, drink to excess (I hope not), but there is no need to suffer physically if you really understand what is needed to play the piano. And in the case of the thumb crossing, there is a rotary mechanism that allows it to move the way the other digits move (see Chapter One) along with the participation of the forearm. No amount of perfection in scales, arpeggios, repeated notes, chords (?) will produce excellence in any particular technical passages in repertoire—necessarily. This is a little like repeating X in order to be able to do Y. If the acquisition of certain techniques is the goal, then I suggest learning them in the music you want to play.

If you are training to run a marathon, then there is logic behind this way of thinking. But, of course, our repetition training is not for building muscle mass or developing endurance. It just isn't. Our repetition training is to work-in, to routine, certain movements that accomplish our goals. And we can achieve these goals easily, without physical suffering by using the body according to its design.

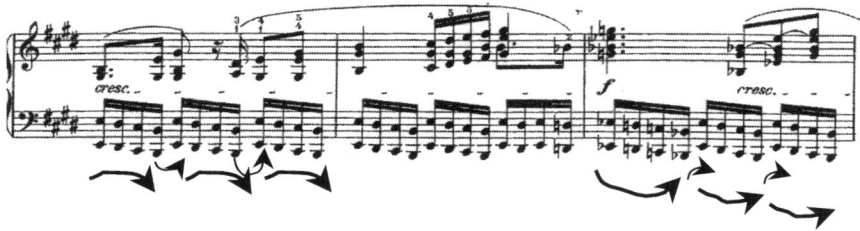

Example 23-1 Chopin Grande Polonaise in A-flat. Octaves.

And now back to our scheduled topic. My favorite example of quick octaves is shown here in Example 23-1, the famous A-flat Polonaise, Artur Rubenstein's signature piece. Already well into his 80's, Rubenstein appeared with the New York Philharmonic in one of their pension benefit concerts. He played three concertos and still the audience wouldn't let him go until he played the Polonaise, which he did with a gracious shrug, but only after much coaxing. But again I digress.

The arrows show the shape of each group of octaves. The E-major section begins with an *over* shape for the first group of four octaves. Then, after a short *under* shape between the group of two octaves, the pattern begins again. When the key changes abruptly to E-flat, the shapes are reversed. Remember, this is a continuous, elliptical movement and for speed, very minimal. Stay in line with the black keys. (Look up the video on YouTube with an excellent view of Rubenstein playing this passage.)

Example 23-2 Liszt Concerto in E-flat. Leaping Octaves.

Leaping octaves can at first seem daunting. But if we keep in mind the principles of our springing action with rotation and add to that the walking arm, leaping octaves become much less challenging. Again, remember to shape and be conscious of the relationship of black and white keys. Staying in line with the black keys usually works best. In this example from the opening of his E-flat concerto, we notice that the passage requires leaping back and forth. How do we do that? Remember how to avoid lockjaw of the arm? Don't try to move in both directions at once. In this case, I recommend grouping from the higher octave to the lower, in groups of two, even in the triplet figure. Do you see why? Practice hint: Start with the first group in measure one, the F. Spring and rotate downward to the B-flat and fall back to the A-flat, landing without playing. Then repeat the formula on the next group.

Here is something else to be aware of. If the torso remains upright, the left hand will crash into it. We don't want any broken ribs. So, the torso must lean slightly to the right before the left hand leaps, remaining more or less equidistant between the two hands as they leap.

TWENTY-FOUR

CO-DEPENDENCE OF THE HANDS

CARE TO DANCE?

The hands very often depend upon one another for cues. One hand will signal the other when it's time to play. Some pianists describe this as a rowing motion. I like Dorothy Taubman's idea that it's rather like choreography. Try this: Put your right hand *in* on the black keys. Yes, that's right, the two short fingers, one and five, will be on short keys. It doesn't matter which ones. Now put your left hand *out* near the edges of any white keys. Notice the difference in planes. The right hand will feel a little higher than the left hand. I've always thought this felt a little like playing the swell and great manuals of an organ, or the different manuals of a harpsichord. In addition to the difference in planes, now notice the piston-like displacement of your arms. Reverse the hands so that the left hand is now *in* and the right hand is *out*. Repeat this several times back and forth like pistons of a motor. Understanding this choreography can be useful when the hands are required to play in close proximity to one another, or just as a matter of basic co-ordination. Remember, one of our over arcing issues in piano playing is the tendency for one hand to try to do what the other is doing. This is a good place to look if a passage feels uncoordinated.

Example 24- 1 Mozart Sonata K545. Planes.

In Example 24-1, notice that the left hand plays *in* while the right hand plays *out*. Notice, too, and I think this is the key to success in this entire passage, that each quarter note cues the entrance of the other hand, that is, right-left, left-right, etc.

Example 24-2 Beethoven Sonata Pathétique. Planes.

If we decide to take the editor's fingering in Example 24-2, which is possible but not necessarily the best, notice that the right hand plays *in* on its first two quarters while the left hand stays *out*. Notice in measure six that the left hand moves from white keys in the previous measure to black keys on the downbeat of six, while the right hand stays *out*. I know, it sounds complicated, but it really isn't. Just follow the pattern of ins and outs, the choreography, indicated in the score and you'll see what I mean. Why does this matter? Glad you asked. In order to avoid a lurch inward or outward, it is important to plan the approach in and out. That is, walk gradually to where you need to be in time to play. It's that simple. And while you're at it, notice which hand is *in* and which hand is *out* at any given moment and feel their placement *together*.

While we have this example up, if you don't mind, let's go off topic slightly. We noticed the *in-out* of the right hand, but what of its relationship to the left? Many students experience fatigue in this passage, which is unnecessary if the relationship between the hands is understood and if the pulse in the left hand is well established. First, let's talk about the pulse in the left hand. This is of course an example of—what, class? Hint: The pattern changes direction with each note. Yes, rotation. Very small. Tiny. Close to the keys. Feel the pulse in groups of four. Feel the pulse in your hand, but don't necessarily hear it, although at first hearing it a little is not a bad idea. But this is not heavy. Ever.

Have you ever been to a fair? Remember the merry-go-round, with its colorful horses on poles bobbing up and down? Please don't bob up and down, but do imagine that the left hand in this passage is moving constantly, with its pulse, like the merry-go-round. Now imagine that the right hand has to jump onto this moving apparatus at just the right spot. Notice now where that spot is in the score. Yes, the hands play together at the fourth beat of measure one. Here's the important point: Feel a starting place, tiny, in both hands where the two begin as a unit. Notice that the right hand plays quarters in two-beat pairs. Each time the right hand moves to a new pair of quarters, feel another start with both hands, again tiny. Teensy. This will help coordinate the passage and eliminate a build up of tension.

Example 24-3 Chopin Prelude No. 3. Plane.

Chopin gives us another merry-go-round. Do you see where you have to jump on? Feel the hands start together there. Notice in the second measure, fourth beat, where the hand moves to thumb on F-sharp. This is the fingering I use. It is a slight adjustment *in*, but don't let that lead your right hand astray. It stays *out* on the white keys.

Example 24-4 Beethoven Sonata Appassionata. Co-Dep.

Look at this tricky passage in the third movement of the Appassionata, Example 24-4. This is a good example of the importance of understanding the relationship of the two hands. Here, the left hand plays from *out* on the interval of a third and in the direction of *in* on the octave. Note: The thumb likes to play in the direction of *in.* As always, very small movements. The right hand plays primarily rotationally. To practice this passage, first feel the in and out of the left hand. Get it moving fluently by feeling slight pulses on the beats. Then feel the rotation in the right hand. Try one beat with hands together, stopping on the first notes of the next beat. Work it in slowly, gradually increasing the tempo.

Sometimes, as we have seen, both hands will be on the same planes, either *in* or *out.* Sometimes they will be on different planes. It is crucial in all of these instances to understand how and when to move and in what direction. By now you will have also noticed that sometimes more than one of our concepts overlap each other, working in tandem.

When the hands are called upon to rotate at the same time, particularly in contrapuntal music, it is helpful to first understand what particular direction is required in each hand as a separate entity and then feel how they coordinate with each other. Here are the four possibilities for combined rotation shown greatly exaggerated. When a coordination problem arises, that is, when one hand seems to be trying to do what the other one is doing, chances are that it is the rotational direction that is in question.

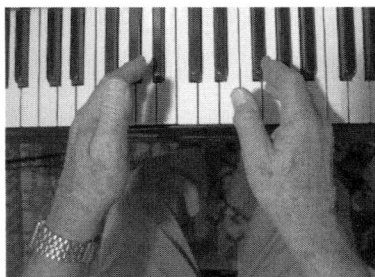

Figure 24-1 Rotate Opposite and Away.

Although the Beethoven example in the third movement of the Appassionata is not, strictly speaking, a rotation coordination issue, try feeling the rotation in the right hand separately. Then feel, slowly, how that relates to the in and out shaping in the left hand.

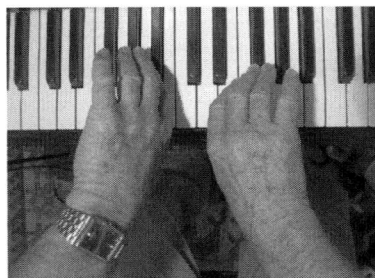

Figure 24-2 Rotate Opposite and Together.

These are advanced concepts and not easy to explain to very young students. If the teacher understands what is required, though, very often a gentle physical nudge in the right direction will solve the problem with a minimum of words. For example, I've had success with ten-year-olds reaching over the shoulders and taking the hands and moving them myself a few times. Or, approach from one side and gently take the hands and place them carefully in the desired positions. I always ask permission first, so as not to startle anyone. Some students might resist the familiarity. Once the sensation is felt, though, very often it will be retained. This is akin to learning to whistle or ride a bike. It's about incorporating a familiar sensation into a different activity.

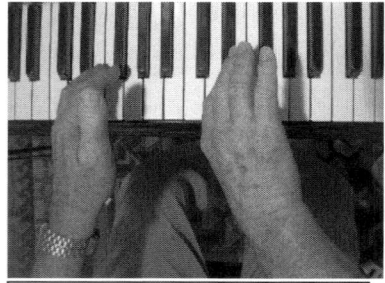

Figure 24-3 Rotate Parallel to Left.

Figure 24-4 Rotate Parrallel to Right.

TWENTY-FIVE

TROUBLE SHOOTING

WHAT'S THE DIAGNOSIS?

I hope I don't break any hearts when I say that the piano is a machine. In an earlier chapter we learned that someone thought of the piano as home to a choir and organ, at which time I expressed my preference for the Philadelphia Orchestra string section. Fanciful imagery can be helpful, perhaps necessary, when developing a musical purpose. It's important to keep in mind, though, that we achieve our musical purpose by means of the expert operation of a system of levers, dampers and hammers, setting into motion more than 12,000 individual parts, a physicist's dream. If you think of it this way, the piano operator must be a very skilled machinist, a mechanical wizard possessed of a remarkable number of refined motor skills. Oh wait. That's actually what we've been discussing.

For a moment, let's think of the operator as a machine, too, a living machine made up of, well, you know what, mostly water. What I think of as the piano playing mechanism, the fingers, hands and forearms—the heart of our operator's machine—is, like the piano or any other machine, subject to malfunction. If the piano develops a buzz or a hammer misfires, we run through our checklist of possible problems, or in my case, call the technician and rely on him to diagnose and repair the problem. If the problem is not the piano's mechanism, but rather the human's mechanism, what then? Warning: Metaphor shift. We call the doctor, describe the problem and wait eagerly for a prescription.

Working in the way I've been describing in this volume is really a diagnostic approach, a term coined by Taubman and particularly apt. Knowledge is our doctor, or until that knowledge is secure, the teacher who has knowledge is the doctor—this book can be the doctor's aide. If something in the technique malfunctions, if there's what I call a bump—a note is not completed, as in transferring of weight—then our interior doctor has to pull out his stethoscope, as it were, and check us out. But, and this is enormously important, he doesn't then write prescriptions for every known medication. He offers the correct one(s) for the particular problem. This is why I don't tell students to play Czerny etudes in preparation for that problem passage, or play the passage in every possible rhythm, or play it 1000 times everyday or just play it slowly. These are vague, general corrections, the equivalent of throwing all medicines at the patient in the hope that one might work. There are many down sides to that general approach, chief among them the likelihood of causing other problems with the unnecessary medications. Remember, first do no harm.

Here, then, is a sort of checklist, similar to the questions a doctor might ask in an examination. Or think of it as a trouble-shooting guide. All operators' manuals have one.

If the hands sense a lapse in coordination, particularly in contrapuntal passages, chances are very good that one hand is trying to do what the other one is doing. The hands can be like naughty children, one daring the other to misbehave. I sometimes think of them as twins who take turns being the evil one. They are mirror images of each other, so in order for them both to *feel* like they are doing the same movement, they must do opposing movements. (Consider, for example, what happens when playing scales in contrary motion.) So, at the spot where the coordination lapse occurs, check the rotation in each hand separately. Do the hands move in parallel or opposite directions? (By the way, this is one of the few types of hands-separate practice that I think is useful. It is a waste of time to learn an entire piece one hand at a time because what we really need to do is figure out how the hands work together.) Once you have determined the direction of the rotation in each hand, then feel the two hands together, slightly exaggerated at first. Then make it very small and work it in and up to speed gradually. This is how we isolate a movement needed for speed, enabling us to practice that same movement slower (see Figures 24-1 to 24-4).

In passages containing running figures up and down the keyboard, always be aware of points at which the direction changes. These turnarounds can throw a monkey wrench into the works. If you detect an issue, that is, do you lose articulation, does the sound weaken, do the fingers feel weak or lack facility? The note at the turnaround spot is an elision; it is the end of one direction and also the beginning point of another direction. Take care, first, that the transition is a smooth and continuous one. Shape *under* on the way up and *over* on the way down, describing a flattened ellipse with no sharp edges. If the elision point is approached by a leap, take care that the hand is compact, that is, don't leave the thumb reaching for where it used to be. Will a walking arm help move laterally? Keep the arm behind the fingers at the turnaround.

If when attempting leaps the piano refuses to play the correct note or if you are suddenly overcome with fear, remember to use the note before the leap as the diving board that sends you the distance, high point over the landing and rotate down into the new spot. The most common reason for the failure to make a leap is the slighting of the note just before it. Notice whether you tend to involve your upper arm when leaping. I mean, does your elbow move outward, away from the torso? If so, this may be a clue; you may be making too large a movement. Our finger-hand-arm unit can be at any angle with the keyboard as long it remains straight with itself. So, in the case of leaps, notice the hinge at the elbow and allow the mechanism to move laterally from there, describing an arc similar to that rounded keyboard we read about. When leaping back and forth repeatedly, does the arm jam, does it get arm lockjaw? If so, remember to group from one direction, allowing it to fall back to the next starting place. This prevents the feeling of trying to go two directions at once.

If the hands tire or feel strain, particularly if the discomfort seems to be cumulative, check for extreme extensions. If the passage contains large, filled-in chords, make sure that the hand isn't gripping and over holding. Play and get off, using the pedal as appropriate to make connections. Other types of extensions have to do with keeping the hand too open in passagework, not taking the thumb along as part of a unified hand, for example.

Every pianist is unique. Every pianist brings a different background and intuition regarding movement at the keyboard. If the music sounds great and the pianist has no physical complaints, then I'm delighted. Sometimes, though, we learn to accept less than the best technical solutions if the musical points come across and we accept these solutions only because we have accustomed ourselves to a certain sensation, not realizing they can be better. This can be a delicate issue. On the one hand, I don't want to suggest changes where none are needed, possibly causing a temporary setback musically. On the other hand, if I see something that I know will become a serious impediment down the road, I feel it's my fiduciary responsibility to point it out. What to do? Well, I encourage the student to ask himself how it feels, describe it to me and then we try, together, to see if we can make it feel easier. You can do this too, for yourself. Be honest. Does this feel easy? Am I afraid I'm going to miss? Do I choke up in the face of what seems difficult? Give yourself a reassuring now, now, there, there and get to work on specific solutions to specific issues. Two aspirin and a call tomorrow won't work.

TWENTY-SIX

THE DILEMMA OF THE DAINTY HAND

PLAYING ON THE EDGE

The octave-challenged hand, when confronting the grimacing sneer of a piano keyboard, seems to shrink to its smallest self in sheer anticipation of being held to the rack for a round of torture. The feeling of being pulled and stretched is a familiar one to those with a less-than-octave reach. It is therefore imperative for those possessed of such a hand to be well tuned to its reports from the dungeon.

When asked about physical requirements for piano playing, my usual answer is that the minimum hand size is an *easy* octave. By that I mean the hand should be able to reach an octave without feeling extended to its extreme. Even better, the hand should be able to play an octave and include a minor second between thumb and first finger without feeling stretched. But experience has shown that, with extra consideration, the smaller hand can be quite successful at the keyboard. And when there is a burning desire to make music, how can I not try to help.

My adult student brought the final movement of Beethoven's C minor sonata, op. 10, no. 1, which, though not in a class with, say, the octave-crazy Liszt Sonata, still has some pesky passages for the smaller hand.

Example 26-1 Beethoven Sonata Op 10, No. 1, 3rd Movement.

First, ignore the editor's fingering. Octaves should be played with five-one always, particularly with a smaller hand. Normally in a passage of quick octaves that move to and from black keys, I would recommend staying in line with the black keys in order to avoid movement in and out. But as we have already seen, octaves feel smaller nearer the outer edge, and in the case of the small hand, smaller is better. So for this student, I worked on shaping and grouping the octaves. For her, the only possibility for playing the passage is to move immediately out to the edge of the white keys after the black A-flat. So she plays two black keys in the first group, two whites and one black in the second group and two whites and one black in the third group. That is, she groups in order to give herself a nanosecond of time get from black to white and back again (notice the lines I've added to the example). This is particularly salient at the end of measure four where she has to move in for only one black octave, the B-flat. Starting a new group after the B-flat gives her a split nanosecond to get back out to the edge, avoiding the feeling of moving two directions at once. Remember lockjaw of the arm? Not good.

Add to this idea of grouping the image of a "U" shape. That is, a movement from in to out, from the fallboard toward the torso, completes the scenario. Every movement is kept to a minimum. Edges are as smooth as possible. The tempo of the movement derives from the velocity of this passage, which in the case of this student may be slightly slower than it is sometimes played, but still respectable enough to make a good case for the drama.

Pianists with smaller hands need to assess carefully the repertoire they play and make decisions based on the frequency of showy octave passages and sizes of filled-in chords. They need to be especially aware of how to re-divide notes between the hands for expedience and how to use the pedal to reduce the amount of time spent holding chords. Clinging to chords is not an option for these hands. But don't despair, many a small hand has negotiated large repertoire. My teacher, Muriel Kerr, had small hands and managed the Brahms B-flat concerto. The distinguished pianist Alicia de Larrocha reportedly had small hands and was able to play big Rachmaninoff pieces, with, I understand, some judicious re-imagining.

TWENTY-SEVEN

IT'S REALLY ABOUT THE MUSIC

THE FOREST FOR THE TREES

Once when I was young and not very experienced, after I'd finished my first graduate degree but before I knew how to play the piano, I found myself in a performance situation. It would be my debut performance in Berlin, a studio performance of my teacher at the prestigious Hochschule für Musik. It was the first time I would be heard in this company and I wanted to make an impression. The occasion was a Schumann evening. My part was to be the Davidsbündlertänze, op. 6, a cycle of eighteen characteristic pieces, not without technical issues and many, many significant expressive opportunities.

I prepared diligently. My teacher, Gerhard Puchelt, was in his element in this repertoire and gave me solid advice and encouragement. "Finally," he said one day, "someone who can give voice to the emotional engagement of Florestan and Eusebius." I did feel a kinship with these two fragments of Schumann's personality, his alter egos. I found the moments of interaction, moments when the two danced together, speaking over and around one another. There were moments of intense introspection, too, in which a tearful Eusebius seemed filled with regret. And of course, Florestan's come-what-may élan often came to the fore.

I drilled over and over again for technical mastery. I tested repeatedly my memory with every device I could think of. Everything seemed in order and the concert came. And went. I played well, I thought. Afterward, Frau Puchelt, ever the diplomat, shook my hand—it's a German thing—and smiled warmly saying something like it was *nice*. My teacher, as I recall, didn't appear at that moment—this might be a repressed memory. My teacher's daughter, a prominent violinist with whom I had often played in recital and a personal friend, offered the following: "I counted the ceiling tiles."

Somewhere about now in this story is where my point appears. The daughter was actually furious. Yes, my friend was angry that I played so boringly and wasted her time. I was shocked and not a little hurt. It hadn't crossed my mind that I might be boring. It was the truth, though, I finally realized after some soul searching. I hadn't seen the forest for the trees. I had been so focused on technique and memory that I had forgotten—yes, forgotten—the point. I had forgotten to practice the music. Along the way in my very diligent preparation I had forgotten to practice performing.

Performing expressively can be exhausting. Not physically exhausting, but emotionally exhausting. It's much easier to solve technical problems and work them in. It is much easier to test the memory by practicing with deliberation, by removing the digital activity from the equation. But to formulate ideas about the music's meaning and rehearse those takes focus and dedication.

Some years ago I read an interview with the great Shakespearean actor Laurence Olivier. His performance as Hamlet became a benchmark in the 1940s and the reporter wanted to know what it was like to be Hamlet eight times a week. Olivier responded that he couldn't be Hamlet eight times a week. It would kill him. It would kill any actor. But what he could do was make the audience *believe* he was Hamlet.

My avoidance of the emotion, then, was understandable. Perhaps my innate preservation instinct kicked in and protected me from self-destructing. I hadn't yet realized that I could, at least to a degree, figure out a technique for making the audience think I was Florestan and Eusebius without actually being them.

So, here's what I've come up with. Here are a few techniques for being someone you're not, for expressing something outside of yourself, or better still, techniques for bringing into the light expressiveness you already have but keep hidden in the dark.

First comes the idea. Verbalize the essence of the music. What is it about? Once I worked with a student on a piece that seemed beyond her understanding. I asked her at one point, if she liked the piece. Oh yes, she loved it. Well, I wondered then what it was about the piece that she liked. This didn't elicit a firm response. So, I moved on. If this were the music of a movie scene, what might be happening on the screen? Her face went blank, yet I sensed wheels turning. When she returned the following week, she exuded the confidence of someone who had an idea. Almost without a word she sat down to play and what emerged was music much closer to an expressive truth. I asked her what she was thinking, what was the idea that moved her. Her response: "It's personal." Well, good enough for me, I thought.

We start with the score. We put to use our understanding of the style, couching our interpretation in what we know of conventions of the period. We examine all of the instructions given us by the composer and try our best to attach a meaning to those instructions. Is a *piano* an actual decibel level or is the composer trying to describe a quality. Does *dolce* mean to play sweetly? How does one play sweetly? Puchelt thought the word *dolce*, especially in Brahms, means to "do something." We have instructions about the lengths of notes, their articulations. But why are some notes shorter than others, even the very same passages. No, I'm not going to tell you the answers. I'm asking you. Think about it. The answers are in you.

Consider the architecture of the line. Pablo Casals made his name as a cellist, the discoverer and first advocate of the Bach solo cello suites. By the end of his life, though, he had become a conductor. In that capacity he recorded many standard classical orchestral works and it was my privilege to perform with him as a double bassist. I think it was his careful study of those Bach works that instilled in him a consciousness of what a line of music can do. For him, a rising line suggested an increase in dynamic intensity, a falling line the opposite. To some modern ears that approach sounded old-fashioned, but whatever your taste, the rise and fall, the shape of the music was clearly delineated. Casals was never boring.

Now it's time for my statement of the obvious. We take the trouble to perfect our technique in order to make music easily and efficiently. Our purpose is to express music, not just depress keys. When practicing the many concepts in this book, applying them to repertoire, avoid the pitfall of missing out on the forest because the trees got in the way.

TWENTY-EIGHT

PUTTING IT ALL TOGETHER

IT'S SENSATIONAL

In a world very distant from our own and separated from us by a warp of time, a boy stands alone—in spirit, if not in fact—quivering with apprehension as Miss Bishop inches her way toward him. The well-worn planks beneath his feet creak with each shift of his feet, the weight of even a ten-year-old sufficient to make them complain. He tries to focus on the elderly upright pianos stationed around the barracks, for this room had at one time housed soldiers on their way to the Pacific theater. He knew, though, that he wouldn't be welcome here. No matter how hard he tried, he couldn't dispel the notion that, yet again, he would be found wanting. He was too young.

Now Miss Bishop had reached the end of the line of children. She stands in front of his mother, whose skirt fortuitously conforms to the fashion of the time and provides ample cover. "How old are you, young man," Miss Bishop asks, poking her head around the obstacle of his mother. Naturally poised as always and mature beyond his years, the boy begins to cry.

So begins a life-long journey of music making, albeit with a pitiful beginning. Miss Bishop broke the rules that summer of 1953 and allowed a boy to remain in a class of twelve-year-olds, the first piano class at the University of Southern California that was designed to demonstrate the benefits of teaching piano in groups. The master teacher was Bernice Frost, author of *The Adult at the Piano*. And yes, the boy of whom I write was I. Still is.

Can you whistle? The musical journey starting that day in a converted barracks became a lifelong pursuit of learning about—and teaching—sensations, although it would be many years before I came to an understanding of the material in these pages. Much of what we learn at the keyboard has to do with learning physical sensations and of learning how to apply familiar sensations to the act of playing the piano. This is why words don't always succeed in helping someone learn these sensations. Whistling is a good example. I can whistle. Here's how: Purse your lips, moisten them and blow. Did that work for you? Perhaps not. This is because whistling requires the acquisition of a sensation that, unfortunately, is difficult to put into words. Riding a bicycle is another example. Both of these sensations are learned through trial and error. In the case of the bicycle, dad pushes until a certain momentum is achieved, then lets go in the hope that the sensation of balance will keep you from crashing. It usually works. Once learned, these sensations never are forgotten. Even after a long hiatus, just pucker up and blow or hop back on and away you go.

Fortunately for us, the piano is less obscure than the two above examples. We can see and touch the piano. We can examine visually what we look like when we move. And yet, there is an element of invisibility, a sensation waiting to be discovered. What does it feel like to walk from one note to the next, completing each note and using each note to propel us to each succeeding note? Try this: Stand balanced on both feet. Now lift one foot as if intending to take a step forward. As you move that raised foot forward, at some point in the gesture you have shifted your entire bodyweight to the other foot. Now complete the movement. Do this again, only this time as you place the raised foot and try to move forward, don't allow your body weight to be transferred to it. This is a stumble, a lurch forward, as if protecting an injured ankle. When we fail to transfer weight from one finger to the next at the keyboard, this lurch—I call it a bump—registers as a disconnect and even if the note sounds, the technique feels imperfect. Over the course of many hours of practice, this bumping can add up to considerable discomfort.

My journey isn't over yet, knock on wood, because I still discover. What began as an intense desire and passed through a fire of fear, came out the other side in the guise of exuberant joy, a joy of music making that persists to this day. I call it the creative urge. It can be a nuisance, a taskmaster, a bane. But it has been my salvation and I hope it is yours, too.

Let's focus now on the word *joy*. If you've concentrated hard, and I know you must have done so in order to absorb the material in this book, you may be thinking, what joy? This is work. Well, there is joy in work, especially if the work leads to personal fulfillment. And that's the point.

Muriel Kerr meant well when she advised me to "get after that" when something didn't work technically. It was the equivalent of pointing out that something is wrong there, which I already knew. What I probably didn't know, beyond mindless rote practice, was how to fix it. When she pointed out further that sound is our business, which I also knew—or would have agreed to if asked—she might have included some instruction as to how to make the required sound. But she didn't. Now I know, and so do you, how to get after a technical deficiency. I know not to accept discomfort or approximation. I know, too, and so do you, that in order to voice a chord or propel my sound into a space I need first to listen with my inner ear, activate my stage ear and call upon the ear in the back row of the hall. The results of this listening are then passed through what I know about producing sound, which is always with the finger-hand-arm collaboration. I know how to feel the weight shift in different degrees to highlight the particular voice required.

When Jacob Gimpel accused me, ever so kindly, of being dishonest, I was at a loss. I know now that he was trying to tell me that even though I was getting the notes and making the musical points in the Liszt concerto, I wasn't yet at a point where it sounded easy. He didn't know this is what he meant. But I know it now. Playing the piano, whether performing in public or in private, as you now are aware, should feel easy. This is not meant to disavow the amount of work that goes into making a performance easy. Not at all. There is work. But I find the work satisfying, now that I know how to proceed. The frustration of having to guess is gone. The mystery is gone. I have knowledge and so do you.

TWENTY-NINE

FIFTY TEACHING MOMENTS

The musical examples that follow have come up at one time or another with students. You and your students may not have the same problems in these pieces, but I offer them here secure in the knowledge that you will be able to apply the principles appropriately when these issues do make an appearance.

BACH INVENTION NUMBER ONE

Example 0 Bach Invention #1.

1. My fingering for the first invention in example one above accommodates the group of notes moving downward together in the scale from A. Notice that the two lines converge, the left hand in slower note values. **2.** Sometimes students feel a disconnect at the top of the scale, where the direction changes first in the right hand and then in the left hand. It helps to feel a down, a mini-start, on the first note of beat three, forth finger in the right hand and thumb in the left. **3.** Again, where the direction changes at the left hand G, it helps to feel a mini-start, a coordination with the right hand's E, which continues in its same direction. **4.** The turnaround on beat four—where the right hand starts a changing note group, changing direction with each note—can sometimes be a challenge too. Here, it helps to notice that the rotation from five to four—G to A in the left-hand—corresponds to rotation in the right hand from thumb D to second finger C. This rotation is parallel to the left (see Figure 24-3).

Hand angle.

Take this E with the right hand.

Example 2 Bach Invention #1.

5. Use the editor's fingering. Notice that in measure one the problem from the previous example is the same with the hands reversed. **6.** In measure three, look at the changes in direction on the third beat. Feel a mini-start in the two hands from right-hand E where I inserted the vertical line. **7.** From the last eighth of measure three, the right hand joins the left in changing direction with each note, making the rotation parallel until beat two of the final measure, where the pattern is interrupted by three right-hand notes in the same direction while the left hand continues the same rotation.

BACH INVENTION NUMBER TWO

Under shape.

Example 3 Bach Invention #2.

8. Shape under for the leaps in Example three. **9.** Keep the hand at an angle as indicated by the arrow in order to accommodate the thumb. **10.** For a clear trill, play thirty-seconds starting from above, E-flat. Of course, the number of notes in the trill will be dependent upon the tempo; ornaments should always reflect the mood of the piece and never be so fast as to sound unclear.

BACH INVENTION NUMBER FOUR

Example 4 Bach Invention #4.

11. In Example four above, group in the left hand after the E, where I inserted the line. **12.** Likewise, group after the right-hand C-sharp. **13.** Notice in measure seven that the right hand changes direction with every note while the left hand plays a scale, notes moving in the same direction. This can present a coordination problem. The solution is as before: Feel the rotation in each hand separately. Then try them together. The starting place is after the tied G. **14.** Group in the left hand after the fifth-finger E, where I've inserted the line. **15.** Feel the same grouping in measure five after the inserted line. **16.** In measure seven, students sometimes have trouble getting started again after the tie. Group after the inserted line, hands starting anew together. Notice the difference in rotation: Right hand changes direction with every note while left hand plays a scale. **17.** There is time for a duplet and triplet in the trill in measure eight, starting on the upper note and ending with C-sharp with the left hand A. **18.** In measure 10, again group after the inserted line, feeling a start in both hands together.

BACH INVENTION NUMBER EIGHT

19. Notice the direction changes in the example below, number 5. The left hand begins a continuous motion, to which the right must attach itself in the middle of the first beat. This is a mini-start to be felt in both hands. **20.** Next, feel the parallel grouping each time the figure turns back on itself.

Example 5 Bach Invention #8.

BACH INVENTION NUMBER TEN

Example 6 Bach Invention 10.

21. In Example six, group after the inserted lines, as well as similar passages as needed, in order to facilitate changes of direction.

Example 7 Bach Invention No. 13.

BACH INVENTION NUMBER 13

22. After a long note as in measure one of figure 7 above, begin finger series again, that is, repeat the same finger if desired.

Example 8 Bach Invention No. 13.

23. In Example eight, first try my fingering. I like repeating the same finger in order to feel a starting place, as in the five to five of the last eight of measure one, although other fingerings are possible. **24.** In the last measure, left hand, notice my fingering again repeats, this time the thumb. I've found that this often helps students coordinate between the hands. **26.** The arrows in measures one and two indicate the angle of the right hand. **27.** In measure three, walk in slightly for the thumb in order to play with five and thumb on the black notes.

MOZART SONATA K. 545

Example 9 Mozart Sonata K. 545.

28. Group after the first 16th note in Example nine above. This facilitates the change of finger from four on the B to three on the C.

29. Coordinate the two-note slur in the right hand with the Alberti of the left hand. Lift slightly from the B and rotate to G. Feel the rotation from D to B in the left hand. The two hands together describe a parallel rotation to the right (see Figure 24-4).

Example 10 Mozart Sonata K 545.

MOZART SONATA K. 331 ALLA TURCA

Example 11 Mozart Sonata K. 331, Alla Turca.

30. Strum the imitation percussion slightly before the beat, using thumb on the last eighth of measure one to leap to five for the beginning of the next strum starting on D. **31.** Finger measure four using thumb on the black key. Walk slightly in starting from finger three.

32. The dramatic moment in measure two of example 12 below often causes concern. Two issues are at play, that is, fingering and letting go of certain tied notes. Try my fingering as indicated, observing the substitutions and let go of the A in measure three. If it's a stretch, the second finger G on beat three can also be released. Repeat the same concept in the parallel passages.

Example 12 Mozart Sonata K. 310.

BACH WTC I, PRELUDE IN C MINOR

Example 12 Bach WTC I, C Minor Prelude.

33. This prelude is one of the few Bach pieces that regularly falls mistakenly into the category of mere etude. Group after the first 16th of the first and third beats as indicated by my added lines. **34.** Notice in Example 13 that the left hand changes pattern in the second measure. Feel the two thumbs on the beat.

Example 13 Bach WTC I, Prelude in C Minor.

35. Rotate away immediately from the left hand A in order to repeat it in the right hand. **36.** In measure two of Example 15, group again after the first notes of beats one and three.

Example 14 Bach WTC I, C Minor Prelude.

Example 15 Bach WTC i, C Minor Prelude.

37. Notice the architecture of the overall line. Melodically, the right hand starts on C, moves down to A-flat, then up to B-natural, C and from the top E-flat a long descending line with suspensions takes us to the bottom of the first page. This is the musical shape of this piece and, supported by colorful harmonic changes and suspensions, should be brought out.

BACH WTC I, PRELUDE IN D MAJOR

38. This is another motoric prelude that often suffers the fate of all etudes, dull and dry. Notice the ample opportunities for shaping groups of notes into longer phrases. **39.** In Example 16, use a rotation from the thumb A on the second beat to get back to four on F-sharp. Likewise, use the second finger to rotate up to A with the fifth finger. In both instances, take care to allow the hand to close. That is, don't keep the thumb extended in the direction of the previous note. The hand will tire in this prelude if kept open fro the duration. **40.** Notice the angle of the hand in measure three.

Example 16 Bach WTC I, D Major Prelude.

BACH WTC I, FUGUE IN D MAJOR

41. This fugue is grand, rather stately, but should not be played in the French overture style with double dotting. **42.** Play

Example 17 Bach WTC I, D Major Fugue.

the thirds in measure two with the left hand, switching back to the right hand on the last 16th. **43.** In Example 17, use rotation to move

Edition Peters.

Example 17 Bach WTC I, D Major Fugue.

from third finger on A to thumb on D. **44.** In measure one of Example 18, play 32nds in the trill starting from above to match the left hand. **45.** On the downbeat of measure two, get off of the thumb D in order to facilitate the 32nds in the left hand. **46.** Again, take the thirds with the left hand, if desired, chaging back to the right hand on the last 16th. **47.** In measure four, use thumb rotation to snap back to the chord on the third beat. **48.** In measure five, start the right hand 32nds with thumb, the next two groups with three-one. **49.** Remember to group the dotted rhythms in the final cadence short to long.

Example 18 Bach WTC I, D Major Fugue.

BACH WTC I, D MINOR PRELUDE

50. This piece is about grouping from the third of three triplets right from the beginning. Notice the arrows in measure one

Example 19 Bach WTC I, D Minor Prelude.

of Example 19. This is both the technical impetus and the musical shape. Notice throughout this movement the melodic inferences in that starting note. Negotiate the leap in measure two by means of a thumb rotation and spring, using the elbow as a hinge. (Remember the circular piano.)

APPENDIX

A PIANIST'S ESSENTIAL LIBRARY, SELECTED

Hafner, Katie

A Romance on Three Legs: Glenn Gould's Obsessive Quest for the Perfect Piano

Hugely talented and famously eccentric, pianist Glenn Gould fought a running battle with a long list of less-than-perfect pianos. *A Romance on Three Legs* is the story of a love that changed Gould's life: his partnership with the Steinway CD 318, a piano whose peculiar action and temperament ushered Gould closer than ever to interpretive perfection. Katie Hafner weaves the compelling tale of Gould, his favorite piano, and the men who worked on it, revealing new details and nuances in the work and mind of one of the twentieth century's greatest artists.

Ferguson, Howard

Keyboard Interpretation From the 14th to the 19th Century: An Introduction.

This standard work is an introduction to the interpretation of keyboard music from the fourteenth to the nineteenth century. Dr Ferguson provides information about the instruments themselves, and discusses this vast, fascinating, and ever-changing subject under the headings: musical types and forms, tempo, phrasing and articulation, fingering, rhythmic conventions, the `tones' or modes, ornamentation, pianists' problems, and editors' problems. It is a clear, detailed, and practical guide to authenticity in performance, which all keyboard players will find indispensable. This reissue incorporates an updated list of modern editions and a completely revised bibliography.

Hinson, Maurice

Guide to the Pianist's Repertoire, third edition.

Guide to the Pianist's Repertoire continues to be the go-to source for piano performers, teachers, and students. Newly updated and expanded with over 250 new composers, this incomparable resource expertly guides readers to solo piano literature. What did a given composer write? What interesting work have I never heard of? How difficult is it? What are its special musical features? How can I reach the publisher? It's all here. Featuring information for more than 2,000 composers, the fourth edition includes enhanced indexes. The new "Hinson" will be an indispensable guide for many years to come.

Keller, Hermann
Phrasing & Articulation

A detailed investigation into the language of music, including in depth discussion of the music of Bach, Mozart and Beethoven.

Loesser, Arthur
Mem, Women and Pianos: A social History

An internationally renowned pianist presents a delightful "piano's-eye view" of Western European and American social history from the 16th through 20th centuries. With wit and erudition, Loesser traces the history of the instrument's design and manufacture and its music, from the clavichord and harpsichord to the modern spinet and concert grand.

Rosen, Charles
The Classical Style (1971).

Analyzes the nature and evolution of the style of the Classical period as it was developed by Haydn, Mozart and Beethoven. Rosen revised the work in 1997, leaving most of the text intact but adding a second chapter on Beethoven and a preface addressing comments on the first edition.

Sonata Forms (1980).

This is in some ways a follow-up on *The Classical Style*; it is an intensive analysis of the primary musical form used in the classical era. Rosen wrote the work when his intended contribution to the New Grove on sonata form was rejected by the editors; he amplified the article he had written into book form.

The Romantic Generation (1995),

This is centered on the early generation of Romantic composers, including Chopin, Liszt, Schumann, and Mendelssohn, and Berlioz.

Beethoven's Piano Sonatas: A Short Companion (2001).

This gives general background on these famous works as well as sonata-by-sonata advice for performers.

Just for Fun:

Critical Entertainments: Music Old and New (2001).

This is a compilation of essays original published in magazines and scholarly journals, mostly the New York Review of Books. It covers a variety of topics, including Oliver Strunk, the work of various composers, the status of contemporary music, and the New Musicology.

Piano Notes: The World of the Pianist (2002).

This is an account of the concert pianist's world, addressed to the general reader. It covers piano technique, the instrument itself, the culture of piano performance, and the repertoire for the instrument. Remember to filter the technical advice through what you know about the body.

Rubinstein, Arthur

My Young Years. New York: Knopf. (1973).

With his uncanny memory, with his unsurpassed gift as raconteur, the adored maestro of the piano at last tells the story of his life: the adventures, the struggles, the amours, the mishaps, and the triumphs... Rubenstein's life and music have been illuminated with a radiant energy, a magic that could only have sprung from a gargantuan love of life. His book—bursting with anecdote, information, opinion, with life—is a testament to that great gift. Illustrated with 24 pages of photographs and mementos.

My Many Years. New York: Knopf. (1980).

Rubinstein's memoir is the continuation of his earlier work

which dealt with his childhood and early adult years. This work covers the years 1917 to 1980. It opens with an account of his South American tour, then goes on to tell of his brief time in New York. It then gives much space to his years in Paris in the 1920's and 1930's. It goes on to tell of his meeting his future wife Nela, their fleeing the Gestapo in France and settling in Hollywood. In Paris Rubinstein rapidly establishes himself as a sought after social figure and mingles with the elite. Above all, of course, Rubinstein is a t master pianist. And he has much to say about the way an artist must use the gift he has been given. This is a rich work and one most highly recommended.

Schonberg, Harold C.
The Great Pianists: From Mozart to the Present.

From Mozart's fabulous legato that "flowed like oil" to Beethoven's oceanlike surge, from Clara Schumann's touch "sharp as a pencil sketch" to Rubinstein's volcanic and sensual playing, *The Great Pianists* brings to life the brilliant, stylish, and sometimes eccentric personalities, methods, and technical peculiarities of history's greatest pianists. Pulitzer Prize–winning critic and author Harold C. Schonberg presents vivid accounts of the artists' performances, styles, and even their personal lives and quirky characteristics—such as Mozart's intense competition with Clementi, Lizst's magnetic effect on women (when he played, ladies flung their jewels on stage), and Gottschalk's persistent nail biting, which left the keys covered with blood. Including profiles of Horowitz and Van Cliburn, among others, and chapters detailing the playing and careers of such modern pianists as de Larrocha, Ashkenazy, Gilels, Gould, Brendel, Bolet, Gutierrez, and Watts, The Great Pianists is a comprehensive and fascinating look at legendary performers past and present.

ABOUT THE AUTHOR

Unlike life, playing the piano is easy and doesn't hurt. This mantra has carried Neil Stannard through what might seem to others like several lifetimes—performing as a collaborative pianist, occasional soloist, symphony bassist and, through it all he has remained a dedicated teacher.

He took part in the first Taubman Institute at, Rensselaerville, NY, and though not a representative of the Institute, he participated in many subsequent institutes at Amherst while studying privately in New York with Edna Golandsky.

He has performed internationally with such artists as David Shifrin, Hermann Baumann, Eugenia Zukerman, Leona Mitchell, Clamma Dale and Christiane Edinger in venues from London to Moscow, including Carnegie Hall, the Kennedy Center, the White House, Vienna's Musikverein, Berlin's Hochschule and Tchaikovsky Hall in Moscow. He has played in the Great Performers at Lincoln Center series, the Berlin Festival, the Vienna Festival, Tage Neue Musik, Marlboro and the Newport Festival. And yes, he has taught continuously.

After graduating cum laude from USC, a scholarship student of Muriel Kerr, he received a Naumberg scholarship on double bass to the Juilliard School (M.S.), during which time he performed in the American Symphony with Leopold Stokowski and in the Marlboro Festival Orchestra with Pablo Casals (Columbia Records). It was also during this time that he made his New York recital debut at Carnegie Recital Hall as a pianist with violinist Christiane Edinger. Later, he studied piano on a German government grant with Gerhard Puchelt in Berlin, completed a doctorate in piano at the University of Arizona with Nicholas Zumbro and for 13 years taught applied piano at the University of Texas at El Paso, where he was a tenured professor. He teaches now in Los Angeles and plays cello in the Santa Monica Symphony.